To Dave + ♡

MW00880011

CRIME
AND CALAMITY

IN YELLOW MEDICINE COUNTY, MINNESOTA

Pat Lubeck

Patricia Lubeck

outskirts
press

Dedication

This book is lovingly dedicated in memory of my dear parents, John and Lorraine, to my siblings – Debra, Doreen, Daniel, David, and Donald, and to my dear departed sisters, Diane and Denise. I am truly blessed with a wonderful family and fond memories of my childhood growing up in Yellow Medicine County. This is paradise.

TABLE OF CONTENTS

Introduction..I

Battle Of Wood Lake 1

Shot By Accident...5

Blizzards, Grasshoppers, And Prairie Fires 13

Gold Rush In Granite Falls..20

Texas Jack...27

Mysterious Death...29

Half An Ounce Of Arsenic...32

A Crime Of Incest..41

Firecracker Starts An Inferno 48

Father Kills His Son 51

A Stabbing Affair..59

A Drunken Brawl..62

Death In A Burning Barn...66

Beaten With A Billy 68

Poison And A Pair Of Scissors 79

Poker Game Gone Bad..81

Raided The Blind Pig 98

The Jail Is Burglarized 102

Strange Disappearance..104

Gambling In A Box Car 107

Froze To Death..110

Train Wreck Near Echo 112

Justifiable Homicide 115

Committed As Insane..117

Burglars Blow Safe At St. Leo 133

Acknowledgments 139

About The Author..141

References 143

Map of Yellow Medicine, Renville, Redwood, Lincoln, and Lyon Counties
In 1874

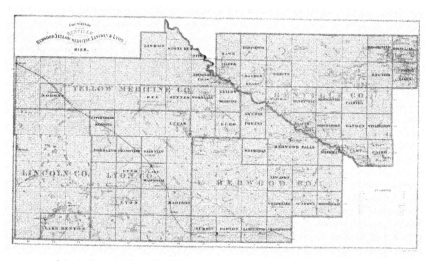

(photo from Yellow Medicine County Historical Society collection)

INTRODUCTION

Minnesota gained legal existence as the Minnesota Territory in 1849 and became the 32nd US state on May 11, 1858. At that point, fifty-seven counties had been established, beginning with the first nine in 1849 – Pembina, Itasca, Mahkahta, Wahnahta, Dahkotah, Wabashaw, Benton, Ramsey, and Washington. Prior to 1849, Yellow Medicine County was under federal jurisdiction and was officially known as a part of Wisconsin Territory. During this time, the territory was mostly inhabited by the Chippewa Tribe to the north and Dakota Tribe to the south. Later, Yellow Medicine County became part of Minnesota Territory and was a part of Dakota and Wabasha counties. According to the treaties of 1850, when tribes of the Sioux surrendered title to their lands in Minnesota, a tract of land ten miles wide on each side of the Minnesota River was reserved as Dakota Territory.

Missionaries quickly moved in after the area was established. In 1852, Dr. Thomas Williamson, a medical missionary with the Presbyterian Church, established the Pejuhatazizi Mission. "Pejuhatazizi" is a Dakota name meaning "Yellow Medicine," the name of a plant used by the Dakota for medicinal purposes. In 1854, Stephen R. Riggs, another Presbyterian missionary, established the Hazel Creek Mission. These two missions were located about five miles south of Granite Falls in what is now Minnesota Falls Township. The government established the Upper Sioux Agency in 1854 in what Sioux Agency Township is now. During the Sioux Uprising of 1862, the agency, missions, and several white settlements were destroyed and because of the uprising the Dakota lands were declared forfeit. Consequently, white settlement began again in 1865. At that time, Yellow Medicine was part of Redwood County Minnesota. The early settlers were largely Scandinavian and German with smaller concentrations of English, Irish, Czech, and Bohemian.

Yellow Medicine County was created by a legislative act on March 6, 1871. The board of three commissioners met on January 1, 1872 in Yellow Medicine City, which became the first county seat. Later, in the spring of 1874, Granite Falls became the county seat. Twenty-one townships and ten communities were established in the new county between 1871 and 1890. The communities included Granite Falls, Canby, Clarkfield, Wood Lake, Echo, Hanley Falls, Porter, Hazel Run, St. Leo, and Burr.

The county has an area of 758 square miles. It is 54 miles long from east to west and from 12 miles north and south at the west end to 21 miles at the eastern boundary. The elevation of the county ranges from 1,739 feet near the southwest corner of the county to 860 feet where the Minnesota River flows out of the county. The mean elevation is 1,165 feet above sea level. The soil, for the most part, is good, black prairie till. Underlying the glacial drift, which covers the entire county, is an irregular layer of igneous gneiss rock which crops out along the Minnesota River in the east end. The land is rich for agriculture and is well watered and drained by the Minnesota River and its tributaries—the Lac Qui Parle and Yellow Medicine Rivers. The county is nestled in between the Minnesota River Valley on the east and the Coteau des Prairies on the west.

Granite Falls is a quaint rural town and is named for the granite and gneiss outcroppings over which the Minnesota River flows. It is the county seat. G.W. Daniels first platted Granite Falls on May 7, 1872. It was incorporated as a village in 1879 and became a city on April 24, 1889. Henry Hill was known for being the founder of Granite Falls; however, it was his brother, Thomas Prentice Hill, who first staked claims to the land on the west side of the river. Thomas Hill was also the first to build here, but in 1868, he deeded the claim to his brother, Henry Hill. Henry also shared a deed to property on the east side of the Minnesota River and built a home on the east side river bluff. Then, with the help of a simple rowboat, he began work on a mill and dam on the west side of the river. When the mill began to operate, it became the center of activity for the small town. The grist mill and its adjoining saw mill processed wheat brought in from local farmers and cut timbers into building lumber. The activity attracted settlers from all walks of life, and soon businesses and homes sprouted up all along Prentice Street.

Creating a community along the banks of a river has its advantages but also has many disadvantages. Crossing the Minnesota River was a major obstacle. A ferry had been established early on, but its capacity was limited, and it took lots of time to move one boat along the ropes. In 1876, the first wagon bridge was built at the north end of town. The bridge served the community well until it was replaced with a steel one in 1911. This bridge was in service until 1975 when it was replaced with the current one used today.

The best-known Granite Falls resident was Andrew Volstead. He was a lawyer who moved his family to Granite Falls in 1886. He first served as the Yellow Medicine County attorney, then as city mayor before becoming elected to Congress in 1903. During his time in office, Andrew Volstead co-wrote the Capper-Volstead Act, which created farm cooperatives. This act is still in effect today.

Granite Falls had its own "lock-up" for its law-breakers at an early date. The jail was a small wooden structure with barred windows on the west and a padlocked door on the north facing the street. The building was located on the south side of Seventh Avenue. The early history of jails in Granite Falls is somewhat obscure. In the summer of 1878, citizens of Granite Falls petitioned the county board to erect a jail. The village was not yet organized into a separate entity, its affairs being governed by the Otis town board. The county commissioners countered with a proposal that if Granite Falls would erect a substantial jail on the courthouse block, the commissioners would issue a county warrant for one hundred dollars, drawing seven per cent interest, to help defray the cost of construction. There was no further development until May 1879, when the county and Granite Falls agreed to build a jail as a joint effort. The jail was to be the property of the county, but Granite Falls was to have equal rights to use it. Cost of construction was $500, and the building was completed that July. By 1892, the jail had deteriorated to the extent that it was dangerous to the prisoners, for they would freeze to death should the night be cold. A prisoner in 1893 tried to commit suicide by cutting his wrist with a sharpened spoon, but the fire in the stove went out, so his blood clotted and stopped running, which foiled his attempt to end his life. By the fall of 1893, a county jail and sheriff's residence were constructed on the corner of Ninth Avenue and Fourth Street, east of the courthouse block. This jail was a superior structure

for its day and was designated a district jail because of its modern facilities. The building was demolished in the fall of 1999; only the jail sign survived. The area was designated as a parking lot for the new law enforcement center constructed in the summer of 2000.

The first county courthouse was constructed in Granite Falls at 365 Ninth Avenue. The citizens had raised enough money for the project and in the spring of 1874, the courthouse was erected. In the spring of 1887, the matter of building an addition came before the Board of County Commissioners but the contemplated improvement was defeated by a vote of three to two. The building of a new courthouse was taken up by the people of Granite Falls. At a meeting of citizens on May 10, 1888, it was decided that the village offer the county $5,000 toward the erection of a courthouse that should cost not less than $12,000 and be completed prior to December 1, 1889. The next day the offer came before the county board, which deferred action until the July meeting. On July 12, 1888, the county commissioners accepted the offer and resolved to construct a courthouse which should cost not more than $15,000 and should be completed during the following year. Frederick E. Hoover of Minneapolis was employed as architect for $800 on November 9, and on January 3, 1889, the contract for the construction of the building was let to C.W. Kerrick & Company of Minneapolis on a bid of $14,769. A building committee was composed of J.J. Mooney, J.A. Thompson and A.J. Volstead.

In January 1889, the legislature passed laws permitting the county commissioners to issue bonds in the amount of $5,000 for courthouse purposes and the village of Granite Falls to issue bonds of the same amount to assist the county. On March 27, the commissioners sold the bonds. The work of construction was rushed, and the corner stone was laid with ceremonies on July 4 of that year. The building was completed and accepted November 23, 1889, and the same day the citizens of Granite Falls paid the $5,000 bonus. At one time, the new courthouse had a wooden fence around it. To the south the yard was low and had a heavy growth of brush to hide two outdoor toilets. The wooden fence was later replaced with an ornamental iron fence in 1899. The old courthouse was eventually sold to George Crandall for $200 and was moved to a neighboring block and made into a nice residence.

Over the years, the courthouse has gone through modernization and expansion, which changed its profile. In 1956, a one-story addition was made, extending west from the north entrance, measuring 24 by 60 feet with a basement. And in 1975, a $417,000 renovation and remodeling job was done, which included the installation of an elevator. Many years later, the courthouse needed major repairs, so rather than put money into a very old and outdated building, the county officials voted to build a new structure instead. And so, in June 2016 a new courthouse was built and the old one, adjacent to it, was demolished. Yet another part of history now gone.

Yellow Medicine County Courthouse built June 2016

Yellow Medicine Courthouse built 1889, demolished 2016
(photos from Yellow Medicine County Historical Society collection)

BATTLE OF WOOD LAKE

THE DAKOTA WAR of 1862, also known as the "Sioux Uprising," was an armed conflict between the United States and several bands of Dakota, also known as the eastern Sioux. It began in August 1862, along the Minnesota River in southwest Minnesota, four years after its admission as a state. Governor Alexander Ramsey's plan, implemented by Colonel Henry Hastings Sibley and frontier commander Charles Eugene Flandrau, was to free European-American settlers held captive by the Indians and to exterminate or drive the Dakota forever beyond the borders of the state. During the war, the Dakota made extensive attacks on hundreds of settlers and immigrants which caused many to flee the area.

The origins of the war extend back to the state's territorial period when white settlers began pushing into the Dakota ancestral homes in southern Minnesota. To preserve at least a portion of those lands for their people, Taoyateduta (Little Crow IV), a leader of the Mdewakanton band of Dakota, and other Dakota leaders negotiated treaties in 1851 that ceded twenty-four million acres to the US government in exchange for a reservation along the Minnesota River and a settlement of $21 million in the form of yearly annuities.

By the early 1860s, with the US embroiled in the Civil War, the annuities from Washington DC were late. With few animals to hunt and no money to buy food, the Dakota faced starvation in the winter of 1862. Soon some of the younger men in the Mdewakanton band began calling for war against the whites to drive them out of southern Minnesota. Little Crow urged caution but eventually agreed to lead the Dakota into battle when he determined that war could not be avoided. The conflict was short-lived, lasting about six weeks during the late summer and early fall of 1862. The white settlers in New Ulm were able to beat back two Indian attacks on the town, but the Dakota achieved early victories at Lower Sioux Agency and Birch Coulee. As the violence continued, Colonel Henry Sibley decided to move his troops closer to the Dakota camps. On September 19, Sibley's troops left Fort Ridgely. Four days later, on September 22, they were camped on the shores of Lone Tree, also known as Battle Lake. (Wood Lake was located three miles away, but its name was later attached to the battle.) That night, a large contingent of Dakota men moved down from their camp near the Chippewa River and assembled near Sibley's encampment. Their plan was to take cover in the tall grass and ambush the soldiers the next morning as they broke camp.

On the morning of September 23, a few soldiers from the Third Minnesota regiment left camp in search of food at the Upper Sioux Agency near Rock Valley Church. Some of the wagons were not on the road and were headed straight at Little Crow's men as they lay in the tall grass. Several of Crow's men got up and fired. This started the fight, and veteran troops from the Third Regiment ran to assist their comrades, aided by the Renville Rangers. They advanced about a half mile from the camp until both flanks were threatened. Sibley ordered Lt. Colonel William Marshall with six companies and an artillery piece to advance and repulse the Indians on the right flank. On the left end of the line, Major Robert McLaren led his men around the lake to defeat an attempted flanking attack. The battle lasted about two hours, during which Chief Mankato was killed by a cannonball. The badly outnumbered Dakota forces had succumbed to Sibley's superior firepower. Knowing that they had been defeated, Little Crow and his men fled into the countryside. The battle was a decisive victory for the United States with heavy casualties inflicted on the Dakota. For his part in the battle, Sibley received a promotion to Brigadier General. Because of the high losses and the death of Chief Mankato, the battle was the last fought by the Sioux in the uprising. Following the Dakota defeat in the fall of 1862, thirty-eight Dakota men were executed in a mass hanging in Mankato, MN. Remaining Dakota, including women and children, were rounded up and encamped at Fort Snelling during the winter of 1862, where they awaited deportation to reservations in Nebraska and South Dakota. Many perished from starvation and illness during their time at the camp.

In 2010 the battlefield site was listed on the National Register of Historic Places as the Wood Lake Battlefield Historic District. It was nominated as the final engagement of the Dakota War of 1862, a watershed period for the State of Minnesota and the Dakota people, and for embodying early commemoration efforts of 1907-1910, culminating in the Wood Lake Battlefield stone monument. The Wood Lake State Monument was established in 1910. It is a fifty-foot granite shaft erected in memory of seven soldiers who died during the battle that took place on September 23, 1862. Both the monument and marker were erected on an acre of the Wood Lake Battlefield which is preserved by the State. The site is located on County Road 18, ½ mile west of Highway 67, between Granite Falls and Echo. The Civil War Trust, its members and partners have purchased and saved 240 acres of Wood Lake Battlefield through 2017.

Colonel Henry Sibley in uniform 1862   **Chief Little Crow c. 1862**
(photos from wikipedia)

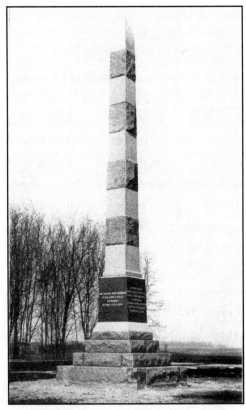

Monument on Wood Lake Battlefield
Erected by the State of Minnesota in Memory of Those Who Met Death at the Battle of
Wood Lake, September 23, 1862 (photo from Yellow Medicine County Historical Society)

CRIME and CALAMITY

SHOT BY ACCIDENT

DAVID WETHERN WAS born in Jerusalem, Maine on March 30, 1824. From 1846 to 1869 he was in business in Detroit, Michigan. His wife, Esther H. Niles, was a native of Penobscot, Maine. In 1869 David Wethern, forty-five years old, traveled the Minnesota River in search of a new location. He had money from the sale of his business in Detroit before he headed west. Wethern met Orange Miller who had a log cabin on the east side of the Minnesota River. One day, Miller rowed Wethern across the river to meet Thomas Prentice Hill, a prominent man in Granite Falls. The two townsmen urged Wethern to make Granite Falls his home. Wethern was impressed with the site and built himself a log home on Oak Street with a small addition on the south side as a store.

In the spring of 1870, Wethern went to St. Paul and bought a small stock of goods which he shipped to Willmar and then hauled across to Granite Falls by team. His store was in a convenient spot, as traffic crossed the river by ferry and went right by his place of business. The Wethern store prospered and its proprietor made two or three trips to St. Paul that summer to purchase more merchandise. By the spring of

1871, the bulk of his inventory had been sold to homesteaders who settled on the land within forty or fifty miles of his store. The stock was so low that Wethern told many people he would have to make another trip to St. Paul for supplies as soon as he could arrange it. This information evidently reached the ears of a young man who was staying in the new town of Willmar, Richard B. Coney, age nineteen, who didn't have much of anything to do at the time. It was May 10, when Coney obtained a team from the Willmar livery to go off on a hunting trip. Coney drove the team into the country and left it with a farmer named Emerson while he walked on foot to Granite Falls. When Coney arrived in that town, he made friends with the storekeeper, Wethern, telling him he was from Willmar and was here on a hunting trip. Wethern said he was going to Willmar in a couple of days and Coney asked if he could accompany him. Wethern agreed.

On the morning of May 15, 1871, Wethern, Henry J. Simpson (Wethern's friend) and Coney traveled by foot toward Willmar. Everyone seemed in good spirits, and all went well. In the evening they met a farmer who gave them food and put them up for the night. On the second day of the journey, May 16, the trio was about nine miles from Willmar and near Emerson's farm when Coney dropped back behind his companions about six or eight feet as they walked through a slough bed to raise some ducks. Coney carried a shotgun and was ready to bring down some ducks. He cocked the gun, brought it to his shoulder, swung around to fire, and stumbled in the tall grass. The gun discharged. The shot entered the back of Wethern's head, and he collapsed to the ground. Death was immediate. Simpson whirled around to see what was going on, when a second shot went off, tearing off Simpson's lower jaw and teeth. Despite the serious wound, Simpson took off running toward the Emerson farm a short distance away. Coney yelled to Simpson to come back and help him do something for Wethern, but he could not stop him. Coney ran to the ox team parked nearby for assistance, but they refused to help him. He then proceeded to Emerson's house, where he found Simpson sitting at the table, bloody and racked with pain. Coney helped Simpson dress the wound, then Simpson got into his buggy and left for Willmar. Coney was found later that afternoon at Emerson's and placed in jail at Willmar. Simpson was taken to St. Paul where he received proper medical attention for his wound.

The preliminary examination was brought before a justice of Kandiyohi County but there was only enough evidence to warrant the commitment of Coney to the county jail. On September 21, 1871, the grand jury of Kandiyohi County indicted Coney on a charge of murder in the first degree. Because of the public's strong feelings against Coney, the defense requested a change of venue to Hennepin County, and Judge Vandenburg agreed. The trial was set for December 1871 at District Court in Hennepin County.

The long-awaited trial of Richard Coney was held on December 12, 1871 at the courthouse in Minneapolis, Hennepin County, with Honorable Judge Vandenburg presiding. The courtroom was full of spectators waiting to get a good look at the young man who murdered David Wethern in cold blood. At 10:00 that morning, the sheriff escorted Coney to a seat next to his attorneys at the defense table. The sheriff removed the handcuffs, but the shackles remained around his ankles. Coney was a man of medium height, slight build, with blue eyes and dark hair. He was dressed in a dark suit, white shirt, and striped tie. He was clean-shaven, except for a small, dark mustache. His dark hair was trimmed and neatly combed. Coney adjusted himself in the chair, leaned over, and whispered into the attorney's ear. His attorneys were Sleeper and Pierce of Minneapolis, well-known, of high caliber, and experienced in their field. The assistant attorney was F. Belfoy, a remarkable attorney in his own right. The prosecution was conducted by County Attorney Clark of Willmar and F.E. Cornell, Attorney General of the State.

The prosecution would present evidence to show that this was a cold-blooded, premeditated murder. There could be no doubt on this point, because the testimony of an eye witness was conclusive, not only about the man who was killed, but also, about the witness, who was maimed and disfigured for life. Star witness for the prosecution was Henry Simpson, the eye witness, who gave all the details of what happened on that fateful day. "After I heard the first shot, I turned and saw Wethern fall to the ground. Immediately the second shot was discharged, and I felt a smarting on my face. Coney pointed the gun at me and told me to lay down or he would shoot. I felt my face and realized my chin and teeth were gone. I ran toward Emerson's with Coney following me, threatening to kill me if I did not lay down. I made it to Emerson's with Coney arriving a brief time later. Coney asked me to forgive him. He said it was an accident, that he was trying to shoot two mallard ducks. Coney did not help me wash my wound. I went from there to Willmar in a buggy which had been left there by me, leaving Coney in Emerson's charge."

The next witness called for the prosecution was Daniel Burr. "Henry Simpson told me about the shooting of Wethern and as I was an officer, I went to Emerson's and arrested Coney that night. I brought him to Willmar and placed him in jail." A few more witnesses were called, and the prosecution rested.

Defense attorney Belfoy would attempt to show that the shooting was purely accidental, that Coney made no attempt to escape, that the gun in question, which belonged to Joseph Emerson, was an old one, so badly out of order that the barrels frequently discharged at the slightest jolt, without even touching the trigger, and that when Coney stumbled, the gun accidentally discharged.

Joseph Emerson was the first witness called to testify for the defense. He stated that he was a farmer and frequently kept people over night. "I last saw Coney on May 16, the day of the shooting. He stayed with me all day until Sheriff Burr came by and arrested him in the early evening. I am the owner of the double-barreled shotgun that I lent to Coney and found it afterwards in my stable. It was a cheap gun in good condition, but the locks went off rather easily. The first I heard of the shooting was when I heard it from Simpson. Coney appeared to feel very badly about what he did but I cannot think of any specific remarks he made."

CRIME and CALAMITY

The final witness called to the stand was defendant, Richard B. Coney.

"Wethern, Simpson and I were walking about a mile and a half from Emerson's. Wethern and Simpson were a few feet ahead. I was carrying the gun with my right hand with a hold of the small of the stock, the barrels extending back over my right arm. There was a small pond on either side of us. I saw some ducks to the left and threw the gun partly into position for firing and at the same time cocking both barrels. When I turned, one of my feet caught in a gopher hole or else the tall grass and I tripped and as I did so, I let go the gun with my left hand and fell when one barrel went off. As I raised to my feet, I saw Wethern falling and Simpson turned around and I saw he was shot in the face. I did not hear the second barrel discharge. Simpson said, 'My God, what are you doing?' I could not speak, I was so bewildered. Simpson's face was covered with blood and he started at once toward Emerson's. I stood bewildered a moment and then ran out to the road where the ox team was. Torgerson was asleep in the wagon and the man who was driving could not speak English. I awoke Torgerson and told him I had shot two men and wanted him to come and see if we could help them. He said he would not fool away his time as he had other business. I then told him I delivered myself up to him as a prisoner, but he said he would have nothing to do with me. I then accompanied the ox team to Emerson's where I found Simpson. I went and got some water and bathed his face. I did not chase Simpson, nor do I remember seeing him after the shooting until I got to Emerson's. I called out to Simpson as he ran, 'For God's sake, let's see what we can do for this man.' But he may have been out of hearing range. I made no attempt to help Wethern. I was afraid to for fear I should get into trouble."

The evidence was announced as closed. The summing up would take place the following morning and the case given to the jury. On the morning of December 15, 1871, the jury found the defendant guilty of murder in the first degree. Judge Vandenburg sentenced Coney to life in prison at Stillwater State Prison. The prisoner was visibly affected by the ordeal and his sentence. At 3:00 p.m., Sheriff Johnson departed for Stillwater with Coney and delivered him to the state prison authorities.

By 1885, Richard Coney had been incarcerated at Stillwater State Prison for fourteen years, longer than any other man. He worked in the machine shop and took pride in the work he did. One day, a local newspaper reporter came to the penitentiary to interview the prisoner. Coney agreed to meet with the reporter to tell his story. "I am here for life on a charge of murder but if ever a man was innocent, I am," said Coney. "I was born in Maine, and my people were of good reputation. It is true that I killed a man, but it was nothing but an accident." Coney showed the reporter a roll of papers he kept hidden in the inner pocket of his dirty, striped prison coat. The papers were the evidence that convicted him. The trial transcript had been copied for him by a friend who believed him to be innocent, and Coney always kept it with him. The transcript included the testimony of a well-known Minneapolis physician who testified as to the nature of the wounds on the deceased. The doctor reported that "the gun must have been in a position not such as a man would hold it, if he intended to shoot another."

Coney said, "I know you are a reporter, but I will tell you one thing, if you will not let anyone know it, for it would hurt other persons—my family." The reporter assured him that nothing would be published that could in any way injure anyone. Coney said, "My name is not 'Coney.' That is the name I took because of my relations, to keep them from any disgrace on my account. My name is 'Murphy' and I have a brother living in Minneapolis." Coney told the reporter, "I don't want you to do anything that is not right, but I wish you would print something about this and go see my brother sometime and tell him you have seen me." Coney told the reporter about his involvement in the prison fire in 1884. "At the time of the fire, when I was choking with smoke, I went up on one of the upper corridors and unlocked twelve cell doors and let out so many men who would soon have burned to death. I did it because I wanted all the prisoners to escape the fire, but I think it should count in my favor if anything does."

The reporter expressed the hope that if innocent, he might be pardoned and promised to mention his case to the public. He shook hands with the prisoner and left the shop, as it was growing dark.

In late February 1885, a bill was introduced in the house of representatives recommending a pardon for Richard Murphy, or "Coney," as he was known. A *Tribune* reporter had interviewed Coney and published his story in the newspaper two weeks earlier. Murphy's (aka Coney) brother lived in north Minneapolis and worked on behalf of the pardon with several other men who had become convinced of Coney's innocence. Even ex-governor Davis believed Coney was innocent. Mr. Murphy had a brother, Edward M. Murphy, who attained the rank of major in the Civil War and came from a good family. He was confident that when the facts in Richard's case were known, his brother would be pardoned.

A document was filed in district court on January 24, 1887 from Governor Hubbard, announcing the commutation of the sentence of Richard B. Coney. The application for his pardon was signed by all the officers of the prison, fifty-eight members of the legislature, ex-governor Davis, and many others. Coney was released from prison in January 1887 after serving sixteen years of a life sentence. He was thirty-five years of age. No further information could be located about his whereabouts after he was released from prison.

After David Wethern's death, the body was taken to Granite Falls for internment. Paul Christopherson Thori was hired to bury the remains. The grave was dug at the foot of a side hill near the Thori home in east Granite Falls. There was no cemetery in the village at that time. Burials were placed on adjacent hilltops. In 1880 the ground was secured for what is now the Granite Falls City Cemetery and it was believed to have been deeded to the cemetery association by Charles A. Pillsbury, the well-known Minnesota milling family. When this was done, the burials that had been made at various places around the city were reinterred in the new cemetery. And so, in the Granite Falls City Cemetery today, you will find an old-fashioned gravestone which reads, "Here lies David Y. Wethern, Shot May 16, 1871." The stone over this grave marks the oldest burial in Yellow Medicine County.

David Wethern's Monument
Granite Falls City Cemetery
(photo by author)

CRIME and CALAMITY

BLIZZARDS, GRASSHOPPERS, AND PRAIRIE FIRES

BLIZZARDS

THE WINTER OF 1872-73 will go down in the county's history as the most severe one. It brought the most terrible blizzard, before or since, in which settlers received their first experience of real hardships. During that long winter, the inhabitants of this part of the state were practically shut out from the rest of the world. For weeks at a time there were no mail deliveries. Many people were inconvenienced for want of food, fuel, and clothing. The sufferings and horrors of that long and dreadful winter were never forgotten by those who experienced them.

January 7, 1873 began the most violent storm anyone had ever seen. For three days the blizzard raged extending over the entire Northwest. The temperature dipped to forty degrees below zero during the entire period of the storm. The air was filled with snow as fine as flour. Through every crevice, key hole and nail hole the fine, white powder penetrated, puffing into the houses like steam. Seventy lives were lost in the storm in Minnesota with thirty-one severely frozen. There was one death in the county and two others were seriously injured.

The forenoon of January 7 started out mild, with a heavy fog over the land. Many people were out and about that day. Some traveled to Willmar for supplies, others visited neighbors, and some went to timber tracts to replenish supplies for fuel. About noon, a great white sheet was bearing down from the northwest. The front of the storm was distinct and in a few minutes a gale moved in at a rate of thirty to forty miles an hour. The air was filled with so much blinding snow that it was impossible to see objects a short distance away. All that night and the following day, the storm raged with a fury. Not until the third day was there any let-up, and finally, by the fourth day, the storm was over. Many who were out during the blizzard lost their way and had thrilling experiences before reaching safety. On the road between Willmar and Yellow Medicine City, five dead bodies were found in a group, and a German farmer and his son were terribly frozen.

There have been a few wintry storms of such unnatural severity that they stand out as events of historical significance. Ranking second was the terrible blizzard of January 12, 1888, when over 200 people lost their lives in different sections of the state. Two lives were lost to this storm in the county, and there were several cases of severe frostbite.

The previous week on January 5, 1888, a storm of sleet had frozen on the surface of the deep snow to an icy smoothness. The day before the storm, the intense cold weather had moderated, the wind shifted to the southwest and there was a heavy snowfall which continued until the blizzard started the next day. On January 12, the weather was mild and by noon it was thawing. A damp snow was falling and there was not much wind. Shortly before 4 p.m., what little wind there was, subsided and there was a dead calm. A short time later the storm came with absolutely no warning. In an instant, a howling, shrieking blizzard was raging with blinding fury, rendering it almost certain death to be caught out in it. The temperature fell rapidly, the storm increased in fury and continued until about 8 a.m. the following morning. It had lost much of its violence but continued until sometime the following day. The storm came at a time when many people were exposed to it, farmers were trading in town, children were dismissed from school and herders were driving their cattle to water. Many cattle were lost in the blinding snow and froze to death. One of the victims of the storm was a 70-year-old man who was coming home from a visit with his neighbor when the storm overtook him. His body was found in a snowdrift two days after the storm. The other death was that of a young boy who got lost and perished near his home, eight miles south of Clarkfield.

The winter was long and fierce and accumulated many feet of snow. For forty-two days that winter, Granite Falls was cut off from the rest of the world. In April, the Minneapolis & St. Louis Railway line was opened after having been closed to traffic nearly two months. Finally, in late spring, normalcy returned to the area once again.

GRASSHOPPERS

Many new settlers arrived in the spring of 1873 to share in the bounteous times which everyone believed would be coming to Yellow Medicine County, but dark days were in store for those who had come here with such high hopes. For several years, beginning in 1873, grasshoppers, or "Rocky Mountain locusts," swept over the country, devouring the crops and bringing disaster in their wake. The people of the county, along with those of all southwestern Minnesota, suffered great hardship as a result. The southwestern part of the state became bankrupt, immigration ceased, and migration began. All who could, mortgaged their property, and many left the state. It was impossible to make a living from the farm; many moved back East to find work, while others attempted to earn a livelihood by trapping. In time, land became valueless; it could not be sold or mortgaged. Bankers refused to consider loans in the grasshopper-infested country.

The grasshoppers first made their appearance in the county in the middle of June 1873, and they did quite a bit of damage in certain parts of the area. Most of the pests departed before long, but enough remained and deposited their eggs during the months of August and September to make certain that the county would be infested the following year. In addition to the grasshopper devastation, the financial panic of 1873 added to the hard times which followed. The loss of crops left some families destitute. Money was extremely scarce, and there was no work for those who had lost their crops.

But the infestation of the grasshoppers was nothing compared to what would soon follow. In 1874, from Manitoba Canada to Texas, the grasshoppers brought devastation and suffering, the visitation being along the entire frontier, especially in southwestern Minnesota, Kansas, and Nebraska. In the spring of that year, the grasshopper eggs which had been deposited the year before began to hatch out during the early days of May, and soon the young pests were attacking the fields. Then, during the early days of July, came an invasion of "foreign" hoppers from the southern counties, which made it evident that the county was not going to escape with the damage done by the "native" species. The locusts appeared in cloud-like formations, drifting with the wind, sometimes entirely disappearing and again returning with a change of wind. The invaders attacked the crops in all parts of the county except Stony Run township, which by some strange turn of fate, escaped the first invasion. There was another invasion on July 15, causing much damage. Before they disappeared, some parts of the county were literally alive with the voracious insects. So thick was the air with the flying pests that at times the sun was obscured. In the evening, when they came down near the earth, the noise they made was like a roaring wind. Those that landed on the prairies seemed to know where the grain fields and gardens were and gathered in them from all directions. Every cornstalk bent over with their weight. The noise they made eating could be heard from quite a distance and resembled hundreds of hogs turned out into the fields. Within a few hours after the locusts landed in an area, entire fields of corn and small grain were completely harvested, as though they had been cut with a reaper and hauled away. It was a discouraging sight. After gorging themselves with the crops, the grasshoppers sometimes piled up in the fields and along the roads to a depth of one or two feet. Horses could hardly be driven through them; even trains were blocked by the nasty pests and had to be shoveled from the track.

The grasshopper plague continued in the county for three more years. On March 13, 1877, a "grasshopper congress" was held in Marshall, Lyon County and was attended by representatives from neighboring counties. Means of contending with the common enemy were discussed and plans were laid out for burning the prairies on a given date with the hope of being able to destroy the young hoppers. Governor John S. Pillsbury set aside April 26, 1877 as a day for fasting and prayer, and on that day, religious services were held throughout the state and deliverance from the scourge was the prayer to God.

The annual dread of grasshopper visitation was again felt in the spring of 1877. The cool, rainy weather of the spring and early summer seemed to have been sent on purpose to give wheat and other grains a rapid and healthy start and at the same time, give the grasshoppers a slow and feeble development. Contributing to the good fortune was a little red parasite, which destroyed the eggs in the nests in the fall and early spring months. These were first noticed in the fall of 1876 and their good work was continued into the next spring. After the young grasshoppers hatched, the parasites attacked them, loading down their frail wings and carcasses until it was almost impossible for them to fly. Bushels of the pests died before they developed sufficiently to do damage. Encouraged, the farmers waged a more determined warfare against their old enemy than in years past. But despite the favorable spring conditions and the war waged by the little parasites and the farmers, many grasshoppers hatched in the warm days of early summer and were soon up to their old tricks. In early July, the grasshoppers brought considerable damage to crops in Wood Lake, Sandnes, and Normania townships, which had before escaped invasion. In some parts of the county, the grasshoppers did practically no damage, and where fields were not molested, an enormous yield of wheat resulted.

The abundant crops harvested in 1877 in portions of the county not visited by the pests, and the belief that "grasshopper days" were a thing of the past, were elements that brought a boom the following year. The settlers began pouring into southwestern Minnesota and parts of Dakota Territory in the spring of 1878. Many of those who once deserted the county because of the scourge returned, and hundreds of others came when it was learned that Yellow Medicine County could produce something besides "grasshoppers."

PRAIRIE FIRES

Those who lived in the county during the early years of its settlement and into the 1880s marveled at the conditions that made a prairie fire dangerous. But conditions in the early days differed greatly from those of the present time. Back then, there were vast stretches of sparsely settled and unbroken prairie, covered with a dense growth of grass, which in the low places, often grew to a tall height. In the fall, the grass died and formed a thick covering of highly flammable material which burned easily when ignited. When a strong wind accompanied one of these conflagrations, the effect was thrilling. The flames would race across the prairie with the speed of the wind, leaping, bounding, rushing along on their fiery way. During the day, the air would be filled with smoke and cinders, and the atmosphere would be hazy; at night, the sky would be illuminated by the blaze, and the bright lines of raging fires could be seen for miles. After the fire burned itself out, the prairie looked like a blackened wasteland.

The settlers were always on the lookout for smoldering fires that could easily burst into a raging inferno in a matter of minutes. Firebreaks, made by plowing furrows around the buildings or haystacks, sometimes served to stop the flames, but with a strong wind, the flames often jumped hundreds of feet, and breaks were no protection.

CRIME and CALAMITY

The favorite method of fighting fires was by back-firing. When one of the fires was seen approaching with the wind, a fire would be set near the property to be saved. This, small at first, could be controlled and wiped out on the leeward side, leaving the flames to slowly eat their way windward to meet the coming blaze. In case of a big conflagration, fire-fighting companies would be organized to go out and battle the flames, using dampened sacks, quilts, or whatever was handy, to wipe out the blaze.

One of the most disastrous fires occurred in October 1872. Great waves of prairie fire swept over most of the county and brought destruction to houses and fields of many of the pioneers. When the fires approached, the settlers sought safety on the plowed fields or along the banks of sloughs and creeks. There they stood and watched with despair as homes and possessions were incinerated. Prairie fires continued to be a menace to the people of the county as late as the fall of 1889. Seldom did an autumn pass without one or more disastrous prairie fires ravaging some part of the county. Prairie fires diminished once the county had become heavily populated and settled.

GOLD RUSH IN GRANITE FALLS

GRANITE FALLS WAS organized as a city in March 1879, and just one month later a "gold rush" occurred within the city limits. The story goes that a group of men, headed by Ed Ault, a Black Hills miner, took shovels, picks, and pans and started out on a prospecting tour for gold. The first attempt happened near Dr. Stratton's residence on Prentice Street in Granite Falls near the Minnesota River, without much success. Then they tried a place further down river, and out of two pans full of dirt, took fourteen pennyweights of pure gold--not much, but great excitement grew out of this small glimmer of gold. Some of the local businessmen pooled their money together and sank a shaft to bedrock, to settle the question of whether there were sufficient quantities of gold to pay or not. Gold fever ran high, considering that the first traces of gold were found in surface washing. This was only the first of several searches for precious metals in the area. The second search for gold took place in 1882, when Williams, Robinson, and Smith spent money to sink the shaft eight feet deep and discovered quartz that assayed at $25 of gold to the ton. But development ceased as the project would not be profitable. In 1883, another lead was discovered by accident on the back part of the lot occupied by A.C. Digen's harness shop and close to the river bank. While digging a "privy vault," a vein of fine-looking quartz was struck, and as Mr. Digen had some experience prospecting in the Black Hills, he continued to investigate. To his surprise, every panful of dirt he washed, brought up more particles of the precious metal. In August 1884, Jonah Peterman, a farmer living near Granite Falls, discovered five or six pebbles of "pure drift gold" within gravel taken from the gizzards of butchered geese. He was ecstatic, but of course, those few gold pebbles were not enough to make him a millionaire.

Nothing more developed regarding the gold rush until 1887 when new promoter, J.M. Thompson, and associates from Kansas City, Missouri appeared on the scene. Thompson came to Granite Falls with a small crew in the spring of that year and began exploration. That summer they sank a shaft to a depth of fifty feet and apparently discovered traces of minerals. A little bottle containing several colors from the mine was on display around town for a week to prove to the doubters that there was gold in Granite Falls.

The initial exploration showed indications of gold in paying quantities and in December 1888, the Kansas City capitalists organized a company to develop the mine. Articles of incorporation were filed with the Yellow Medicine County Register of Deeds and the Ben Harrison Silver and Gold Mining Company of Granite Falls was formed. It was capitalized at $125,000 in stock, divided into 5,000 shares at the value of $25 each and the purpose was to carry on mining business in the town. The organizers were all non-residents, except for Gorham Powers, a well-known attorney in town and later appointed judge. J.M. Thompson was appointed president of the newly organized company.

In May 1889, The Ben Harrison Company set up their equipment and started drilling the shaft. It wasn't long before the shaft was at forty feet and showing better at every foot. An expert from Helena, Montana was at the site and declared the prospects could not be better. A genuine gold boom had struck this place, and the town was in a frenzy. No such enthusiasm had ever been known before. Mr. Thompson was associated with men of means who were acquainted with mining and who had confidence that the newly developed mine would produce an abundance of wealth.

J.M. Thompson met with citizens of Granite Falls at the Engine House in June 1889. The building was packed, the stairs were loaded, and many stood outside eager to hear what would be said. Mr. Thompson addressed the assembly in a plain and practical manner, producing documents showing affidavits of assays made by several different smelting companies regarding the richness of ore taken out of the mine. He proposed that the mine would rival many in the famous mining districts of Montana, Colorado, the Black Hills, and even California. About 1,100 shares of this stock were sold in Kansas City during the winter and early spring. Thompson set aside 150 shares to be sold that night, and in only eight minutes, all had been purchased. Thompson promised that within six weeks Granite Falls would be a full-fledged mining town. He declared, "In one year from now, and basing my assertion on what I know of the ore here, I tell you, your agricultural interests will be equaled or exceeded by your mining industries." The people were fairly convinced that gold, in paying quantities, existed and that every dollar invested would yield a bountiful harvest. The rock formation that existed here was similar in nature to that of the Black Hills, where millions of dollars in wealth had added to the commerce of the country. The mammoth upheaval that existed in this valley was a phenomenon unexplained by geologists and a puzzle to theorists. The ore in the Ben Harrison had steadily increased in richness below sand level, and now at a depth of sixty feet, ore was taken out that was equal in value to several rich mines in this country.

During the summer of 1889, the Ben Harrison Company was hard at work; every blast seemed to open richer quartz and in larger quantities than the preceding one. Scores of visitors viewed the shaft, and a few of them ventured to the bottom. Samples of ore were carried away by everyone who was brave enough to trek to the bottom of the shaft. Gold fever was by no means confined to the male population. One lady was the fortunate possessor of ten acres of land or rock amid the supposed best gold-bearing district. Its value a few weeks prior had been about $10 per acre, but now, it was not for sale.

Thompson thought the vein they were currently developing had a general trend east and west, and this was probably the case with other veins recently discovered. Thompson proposed to go down fifteen to twenty feet further before blasting laterally, and by the ring of hammers, the force was doubled. He planned on installing a pump to keep the drills going as much as possible. The Ben Harrison Company was proving to be a good paying investment. All summer, miners were employed bringing ore to the surface, but by late July of that year, there were reports of ore being stockpiled at the site and stock selling at par value. On August 6, 1889, the last shipment of ore was made from the Ben Harrison Company, but no record was available as to its value. Soon activity ceased entirely, and the promoters disappeared. The boom died and was never revived to any considerable extent since then.

It was uncertain whether the promoters were out to fleece the public from the very beginning or not. They had done considerable work before organizing a company, having sunk a shaft to the depth of fifty feet the previous year. It was possible that the promoter had sunk all his capital into the project sincerely believing he had a good thing. On the other hand, it might have been a scheme from the start "salting" the shaft with gold-bearing ore and reluctantly selling shares. Whatever the true story, many a strongbox contained shares of the Ben Harrison Company stock, and the unfortunate buyers quietly forgot their losses and turned to other methods of gaining wealth. The Ben Harrison mine shaft was eventually filled in but not before another bit of history was added to it.

In June 1896, Norman Jensvold, the fourteen-year-old son of Sheriff Jensvold of Granite Falls, was approached by a man who asked him what he would take for his watch. Jensvold told him "$5." The boy followed the stranger to his tent half a mile below town to get the money. They walked along until reaching a point near the "old gold mine," when the stranger ordered Norman to give him everything he had in his pockets and to take off his coat. Then he began pounding and kicking Norman and said, "If I let you go, you will give me away." Norman begged the man not to kill him, but he continued to kick and pound the boy until he thought he was dead. He dragged Norman into some bushes near the old mine shaft and covered him with brush and stones, and then left. Sometime later, Norman crawled out, not knowing how badly he was injured, and made his way home. The boy's injuries were serious but did not prove fatal. On hearing the story from his son and seeing the condition he was in; the sheriff could hardly contain himself. He reported the situation to the marshal and blew the whistle, calling the people together for the manhunt.

George Wells, a farmer from the area, told Sheriff Schwalier of Canby about a suspicious man with three fingers missing from his left hand, rather gawky-looking, who rode with him from near Porter the day before. This raised suspicion in their minds that he was the fellow they wanted. Wells and the sheriff went to the barn, where it was reported the stranger had lodged the night before. When the men reached the barn, a head was seen in the window, and without a doubt, they had found their man. After deciding with others in the manhunt to secure the area, the two men boldly went into the barn and climbed the hayloft where the man was quietly sleeping. The sheriff roused the man and said, "What is your name and where are you from?" The man replied, "My name is Albert Hillman and I live four miles south of Porter. I'm nineteen years old." Schwalier told him he was his prisoner and to come along with him. The two brought the fellow to the jail, where Sheriff Jensvold lived and took him before Norman to be identified. The curtain was raised and in an instant the boy said, "That is the man." Hillman was placed in a cell, and again the whistle sounded to advise those out on the manhunt to abandon it. Not less than one thousand people visited the jail to see the heartless wretch incarcerated. He brazenly talked to them, denied he ever saw the boy before and spoke lightly of the affair.

On being searched, Hillman had three jackknives and a watch found on his person, as well as, some other trinkets but not the boy's watch. The prisoner told his side of the story: "I was down below town in the forenoon and met a party who offered me 25 cents to bring him a boy having a watch and other things of value on his person. I found this one and took him down to where I had agreed to meet this stranger and found him waiting for me. I demanded the 25 cents and he told me to scare the boy, so he would give up what he had. This I did by shaking him when the man told me to leave or he would kill me. I dropped the watch upon the ground and ran almost directly to the barn where I was arrested. I am not guilty of beating the boy." This was just one story told by Hillman, but he had told so many lies regarding the affair that people gave little credence to what he said.

Later, a hunt was made for the boy's watch, and the searchers were rewarded by finding it, with some other trinkets taken from the boy, under a step leading into the barn where Hillman was arrested. The chain of evidence was complete against Hillman.

A large crowd gathered on the outskirts of town and talked very threateningly of taking the prisoner out and lynching him. The authorities became aware that trouble was brewing and the deputy sheriff, accompanied by Andrew Mikkelson on an order from the county attorney, took the prisoner to Sacred Heart, Renville County, where the three boarded the eastbound train for Minneapolis. The prisoner was placed in the Ramsey County Jail for safe-keeping. Two weeks later, after things had cooled down, Hillman was returned to the Granite Falls Jail to await the action of the grand jury. Hillman practically confessed everything and left no room for doubt regarding his crime. He did not seem to realize the seriousness of the offence with which he was charged.

In March 1897, Hillman was brought before the court to be tried for his attempted murder of the Jensvold boy. He changed his plea from "not guilty" to "guilty" so that all the judge had to do was sentence him. Hillman, no doubt, intended to kill the Jensvold boy and thought he had. The judge sentenced Hillman to fourteen years at Stillwater State Prison. He took his sentence as a matter of course and seemed to feel more at ease after it was pronounced than he did before.

Norman Jensvold made a full recovery from his injuries and never befriended any strangers who might cross his path ever again.

Sometime later, the Ben Harrison mine shaft was filled in to deter any future crimes from being perpetrated near that place. This finally ended the whirlpool of excitement that once existed when gold was first discovered in the village of Granite Falls.

TEXAS JACK

HORSE THIEVES WERE numerous and formidable on the frontier, and although today we can laugh at the severity with which horse stealing was punished, the reasons are evident. Horses were the most valuable property of the frontiersmen, whether cowboy, hunter, or settler, and were essential to his well-being and even his life. Horses were always marketable and easily stolen. Thus, horse stealing was a tempting business for the reckless ruffians and was always followed up by armed men. It was not uncommon for vigilantes to shoot horse thieves on sight or leave them hanging from the nearest tree.

The escape of John Wilbur, alias "Texas Jack," from Hennepin County Jail on May 14, 1881, caused much excitement. A large amount of money had been spent in making this jail a safe place for the keeping of criminals. Notices of the safe and secure condition of the cells and jail, and the care bestowed by the officials to whom prisoners from other counties were committed for safe keeping, were mailed out

27

to various parts of the state in April 1881.

Sheriff Fortier of Yellow Medicine County arrived in Minneapolis with three delegates for the penitentiary at Stillwater. One of the three was John J. Wilbur, who was to serve out a three-year sentence for horse stealing in that county. Texas Jack was a desperate character and was captured in November 1880 at Yankton, South Dakota. He had been convicted in Yellow Medicine County and was to serve out his sentence at Stillwater State Prison.

Owing to the incapacity and carelessness of Mat Bros and John Euch, the two jailers at the Hennepin County Jail, Wilbur escaped, and Sheriff Fortier was very cranky and disgusted over the whole affair. Although Sheriff Eustis of Hennepin County was not individually responsible for the escape of Wilbur, yet by the employment of intelligent and capable men as jailers, such an occurrence would have been avoided. It may be stated that since Bros and Euch had been in charge at the jail, only sixteen prisoners had escaped. This fact should have had them discharged at once and suitable men hired. Thanks to the incompetence of these two jailers, Texas Jack made an easy escape from this safe and secure jail. A reward of $100 was offered for his arrest, but Texas Jack was never seen in these parts again.

MYSTERIOUS DEATH

IN MAY 1885, Clarence Cook and Rube Morrison left Rochester, MN for Minneapolis where they formed a partnership and started a bakery. They continued in business there a couple of weeks, and by the third week, Cook left Minneapolis for Canby where he had formerly resided, with the intention of hunting and fishing for a few days before returning home.

On June 11, Cook sent a keg of fish to his family in Rochester and on the following day, June 12, borrowed a gun and went out hunting plover (a small type of bird) to send to his wife, who had been ill for some time. He left Canby about 9 a.m., alone, having been unsuccessful in getting a companion to go with him, and went out on the prairie. A man was near him most of the forenoon with a herd of cattle, but Cook and the herder got separated, and at about 3 p.m. as the herder was bringing his cattle into town, he saw Cook lying on the ground and his dog sitting near him. The herder went near enough to ascertain what the trouble was and then went to town and gave the alarm. A doctor was summoned, along with others, who arrived at the scene and found Cook lying on his face, dead. An examination showed that a charge of shot penetrated the breast, a portion of which passed into the heart.

It appeared the shooting was purely accidental; Cook was sitting down, and it was thought, pulling the gun toward him, when the hammer caught on something and the gun discharged. The gun, a double-barreled, breech-loading shotgun, was found lying a little distance from him with one barrel discharged. Death was instantaneous. The body was carried to town and properly cared for. Cook's friends and relatives were notified of the tragedy. The following afternoon, the body was taken to the train station by the Masons and Odd Fellows. Colonel Strong and S.T. Bland accompanied the remains to Rochester.

It was first thought that Mr. Cook killed himself, but this did not appear to be the case. That morning, he asked several of his friends to go with him, but they were busy and could not go. He would not have wanted anyone along if he had intended to commit suicide. The theory was that he had laid his gun on the ground and seeing a bird, grabbed the gun by the muzzle and dragged it toward him. The hammer caught in the grass and then came down with sufficient force to fire the gun.

Cook was known to be a very careless hunter. About a year previous, while out hunting, he stood holding upright a gun loaded and cocked, waiting for the dogs to set some birds. His own dog came toward him and jumped upon him. Not removing the gun from its dangerous position, he ordered the dog down, when its claw caught the trigger and discharged the gun, which tore off the front of his hat and greatly alarmed the men he was with. This is only one of the many incidents of his carelessness while hunting. All the people who were at the scene and examined the surroundings, surmised that it was a tragic accident and not a suicide.

Mr. Cook had a large circle of friends, both in Rochester and Canby who were pained to learn of his death. He was thirty-four years of age. He left a wife and five children. He was a member of the Masonic and Odd Fellows Lodges of Canby and the body was escorted to Rochester by a delegation from those lodges. He was buried in the Oakwood Cemetery in Rochester with the Odd Fellows conducting the service.

CRIME and CALAMITY

Clarence P. Cook's Monument
Oakwood Cemetery, Rochester, MN
(photo from "Find a Grave")

HALF AN OUNCE
OF ARSENIC

In a July 1885, edition of the *Granite Falls Tribune* it was reported: "John Purvis, aged 55 years died of heart disease on July 16, 1885." But several little incidents that happened before the death of Purvis led some to believe that he did not die a natural death. There was considerable talk of instituting an examination before the funeral, but as the county attorney was absent, the funeral would proceed. Because of the suspicious death of John Purvis, the coroner of Chippewa County was notified, along with Dr. Rogers of Montevideo.

Since the burial of Purvis, it had been discovered that two days before his death, his wife, Sarah, had purchased half an ounce of arsenic at a drug store, which confirmed the first suspicions, and it was deemed advisable to exhume the body and search for poison. The proper officers, accompanied by Drs. Stratton and Rogers, and many spectators, went to the graveyard north of Granite Falls. The body of Purvis was taken up and placed in a tent set up for the occasion. A jury was empaneled, and after some testimony, a post mortem examination was made. The internal organs all showed evident signs of poison of some kind. But an entirely new phase of the case was brought forth by the finding of copious quantities of quicksilver scattered all through his organs and intestines. The question was: How did it come to be there?

Finally, a jury on the testimony of the doctors and the evidence before them, brought in a verdict of "death by violence," and Sarah Purvis was arrested. A guard was left to watch her at her house. The preliminary hearing for Mrs. Purvis was held in August 1885 at the Granite Falls courthouse. Messrs. Shannon & McLarty appeared for the defense, and J.W. Arctander and Gorham Powers for the State. The prosecution brought forth the following witnesses:

James A. Dodge, chemist at the State University in Minneapolis was the first witness called. He testified to having made a chemical analysis of the liver of Mr. Purvis and found sufficient arsenic, in his opinion, to cause death.

Dr. Rogers of Montevideo was next sworn and gave his opinion that Purvis did not die a natural death and gave his reasons for such belief.

J.G.C. Johnson testified that Mrs. Purvis bought poison from him, referring to his record book, on July 14.

Dr. Stratton testified to exhuming the body and procuring the liver, which he delivered to the chemist.

R.R. Hotchkiss testified to having gone to the house of Purvis shortly after his death. He was present at the post mortem examination, saw the body exhumed, and identified it as the body of John Purvis.

Frank Dillingham was next sworn and said he was at the house shortly before Purvis died and saw Mrs. Purvis give him medicine. He saw Purvis' body at the funeral and at the coroner's inquest.

This concluded the prosecution. The defense offered no evidence. The man was poisoned, and the circumstances surrounding the tragedy would indicate that this was the case. The prisoner showed no signs of remorse and seemed to treat the affair with indifference. Justice Lewis concluded that he had sufficient evidence to retain Mrs. Purvis and remanded her to jail to await the October term of the district court.

On December 1, 1885, Mrs. Purvis, who had been confined in the county jail since the previous spring on the charge of poisoning her husband, and who pled "not guilty" at the regular term, was arraigned. Her attorney C.E. Shannon, by her request, wished to modify the plea to "guilty of murder in the second degree," which was accepted by the court, and this ended the trial, so far as she was concerned. Witnesses for the prosecution were notified by telegraph that they were not needed, and the crowd, who had expected to hear the case, were sadly disappointed. The case was placed in the hands of the judge for final disposal. Sarah Purvis was brought in and stood before Judge Brown while sentence was pronounced: "Stillwater for life at hard labor," was the decree of the court. The following day, Sheriff Fortier, accompanied by his wife, and Deputy LeSuer, with the prisoner in charge, started for Stillwater, where Purvis would spend the rest of her life. But her story does not end here.

Judge Gorham Powers wrote a letter to Governor William Merriam on April 22, 1892.

Dear Sir,

The undersigned citizens of Yellow Medicine County respectfully represent that they are acquainted with Mrs. Sarah C. Purvis, now serving a life sentence for murder in the State Prison at Stillwater in this State. That they are acquainted with the circumstances of her trial and conviction. They also state that in their opinion she was not wholly to blame for the crime for which she is now serving her sentence, but that outside influence was brought to bear by other parties. They believe that society would be perfectly safe if she was released and that the needs of justice have been fully satisfied and they respectfully petition you that she may be pardoned.

Signed Gorham Powers, District Judge.

CRIME and CALAMITY

This letter included the signatures of eleven other notable men from the county.

Then on March 20, 1893, Sarah Purvis' attorney C.E. Shannon wrote a letter to then Governor Knute Nelson regarding the pardon.

Dear Sir,

Myself and D.A. McLarty of Granite Falls were attorneys in 1885 for Mrs. Purvis who was indicted for murder. She was convicted of murder in the second degree and sentenced for life in December of that year. She has now served nearly eight years. There were peculiar circumstances concerning the case which could not properly be brought before the court at that time as a defense but which in my judgment would be proper for you to consider in the application for the pardon which I am informed today has been made through her friends and some of the citizens of Granite Falls. I can briefly say here that I investigated the thing very thoroughly at the time and became satisfied beyond the possibility of a doubt that she was urged into the matter by one, Henry Howard, who went even so far as to arrange all the details of the crime himself, but the evidence unfortunately was of such a character that it only pointed toward Mrs. Purvis. I laid the entire matter before the County Attorney at the time, who is now Judge Powers, and sought Howard indicted and punished, as well as, Mrs. Purvis. The only trouble was that as I said before, what evidence could be obtained only pointed toward her, so that it was so far as prosecution was concerned, to have been solely upon her evidence as an accomplice, which as you are aware would not be sufficient to convict and Mr. Powers, as I think now and thought then, very properly declined to attempt a prosecution of Howard. I explained the matter fully to Judge Brown who was then presiding judge and he agreed with Mr. Powers that there would not be sufficient evidence to convict Howard. I knew Mrs. Purvis sometime before the crime was committed and also have taken pains from time to time to inquire of the prison authorities as to her conduct in prison, and I have always known her to be exemplary in her conduct as a citizen both before and since in prison, and I am sure that the ends and aims of justice have been met by her punishment, and that society will be perfectly safe if she is released, which I think ought to be done and let her spend the balance of her days with her two sons. If you desire any further or more detailed information than I have given and if you will indicate that you so desire, I will come to St. Paul and confer with you in the matter.

Signed yours very truly, C.E. Shannon.

Gorham Powers wrote another letter to then Governor Knute Nelson on March 24, 1893. In this letter he described his position as prosecuting attorney at the time Mrs. Purvis was convicted. From his thorough investigation of all the facts and circumstances, he believed another party was involved in the murder of John Purvis.

At the time of the murder, a man by the name of Henry Howard lived in the house and with the family of John Purvis. From Howard's subsequent career with another family in this city, I have become convinced that he was the instigator of the crime. This may be no excuse in point of law, but in point of real guilt, and in the matter of executive clemency, it would seem to have great weight.... I hope a pardon may be granted.

Signed yours respectfully, Gorham Powers.

By 1897, Sarah Purvis still patiently waited to receive word of her pardon. She had now been twelve years in confinement in the state prison. When she went to prison, her son William was nine, and Ernest was seven. The two sons lived with their uncle, Isaac Hoyt, while their mother was incarcerated. The boys loved their mother and did everything they could to get her released from prison. They were now ages twenty-one and nineteen and looked forward to a happy reunion with their mother upon her release from prison.

County Attorney A.J. Volstead wrote a letter to the Board of Pardons in St. Paul on January 2, 1897. In the letter he stated that he firmly believed:

> ...She (Sarah) was impelled to do the act by a person with whom she then sustained an improper relationship, and that it was not her planning or voluntary act that affected the murder. ...
> Signed respectfully yours, A.J. Volstead, County Attorney.

On December 28, 1897, the Board of Pardons notified County Attorney Volstead that they would meet the following month to consider the application for the pardon of Sarah Purvis. After the Board of Pardons reviewed the case, Sarah Purvis was pardoned on January 3, 1898 after serving 13 years of a life sentence. Sarah was very happy to be reunited with her family and moved with relatives somewhere in the South. Sarah remained a widow and passed away on February 7, 1928 at the age of seventy-eight. She died of capillary bronchitis and was buried in the Riverview Cemetery in Kalamazoo, MI.

Henry Howard, the real perpetrator of this crime, got away with murder. In this case, the justice system failed Sarah Purvis. She spent thirteen years of her life in jail for a crime she was only partly responsible for. Howard, as an accomplice and appearing to be the real instigator in this matter, should have seen his day in court, but that was not the case. To this day nobody knows why Howard was never convicted for his part in this crime or where he fled to after the murder was committed. It appeared Howard was a shady character and a real con-man.

The Purvis family was plagued with another tragedy years later. Sarah's grandson, Ernest Jr., died of injuries he sustained in a robbery. On January 3, 1972, Ernest, a clerk at the Stanley Hotel in Kalamazoo, MI was robbed of $20 and hit over the head with a gun. Two men approached the hotel desk and demanded money from Purvis. Ernest gave them $11 from the hotel and $9 of his own. Purvis resided at the hotel. For some reason, one of the robbers hit him over the head with a small handgun. Purvis was treated with stitches at Bronson Hospital in Kalamazoo after the holdup. Later, he went to visit his daughter in Gobles, MI. Purvis was not feeling well and went to the Lakeview Hospital in Paw Paw, MI on January 10, 1972. He was immediately transferred to Bronson Hospital and died later that day of a massive blood clot in the brain caused by being struck in the head at the holdup. Ernest Purvis was forty-nine years old and was buried in the Robinson Cemetery in Kalamazoo, MI.

John Purvis' Monument
Granite Falls City Cemetery
(photo by author)

CRIME and CALAMITY

Sarah Purvis' Monument
Riverview Cemetery, Kalamazoo, MI
(photo from "Find A Grave")

Sarah Purvis with granddaughter Marie, c. 1920s
(photo from relative, Marilyn Sprague, Gobles, MI)

A CRIME OF INCEST

OLE O. NARKIN married Martha (maiden name unknown) in October 1863 in La Crosse, Wisconsin. They eventually moved to the town of Wergeland, Yellow Medicine County and homesteaded a farm there for about fourteen years. They had seven children, six girls and one boy. Ole and Martha had a hard life, raising a large family and farming the land. After twenty years of marriage, it seemed things were not working out well for the couple. One day, three daughters, Martha, Emma, and Sarah told their mother that their father had been having improper relations with them. Martha, the mother, was devastated hearing this ugly news and reported it to the authorities.

Ole Narkin was indicted by the Grand Jury at the May term of district court in 1885 with the crime of incest. Indictment No. 1 with Martha Narkin was on July 2, 1883. Indictment No. 2 with Martha Narkin was on August 14, 1884, and the third indictment was the same charge with Emma Narkin on July 2, 1883. After the indictment, it appeared Narkin left the area, and nobody knew where he went. He often spent time in the Dakotas working for farmers during the threshing season. A warrant was issued for Narkin's arrest. Sheriff LeSuer notified all postmasters in towns where he thought Narkin might stop, to keep a lookout for him, in case he called for mail. Narkin made an appearance at the Estelline post office, somewhere in Dakota territory. He was followed into the country and found living with a farmer. Someone sent a telegram to Sheriff LeSuer, notifying him that Narkin had been spotted. LeSuer got a team and drove to the place where Narkin had been working on a farm. The sheriff had developed the best qualities as a detective, in tracking and capturing his man. In May 1885, Sheriff LeSuer of Canby arrested Narkin and brought him back to Granite Falls where he was placed in jail. He would remain there until court convened in the fall, unless he could furnish the $2000 bail, which was not likely.

Narkin was tried at the October term of court. He pled "not guilty" and the case was ably argued by both sides. A jury of twelve men was impaneled. His daughters all testified strongly against him, satisfying both the jury and spectators that the inhuman monster was guilty of the offense charged. The jury went out and deliberated but a few minutes and returned the verdict of "guilty." The judge told Narkin to stand and hear his sentence, often allowing him to say what he wished on behalf of himself. Narkin made a few rambling remarks, trying to implicate other parties, and expressed his belief that the whole affair was a "put up job" on him. The judge sentenced Narkin to hard labor at Stillwater State Prison for two years on the first count and one year and six months on the second count. The third count would still hang over him to indemnify the public for his future behavior. The daughters did not wish to see their father, but he insisted that he must see them. His request was denied by the district attorney.

The following letter was received by Narkin while in jail in Granite Falls, and after being translated from German into English by K.T. Hazelberg, was submitted for publication. The language used was almost precisely like the original letter, showing the esteem that Narkin was held in by his wife and family. His four daughters, now nearly grown, had reason to feel grateful to the community for the interest taken in bringing their profligate parent to speedy justice. The letter appeared in the *Granite Falls Tribune*, dated December 8, 1885.

Ole Narkin, I will now answer your letters. It is not an easy matter to answer them. You say you hear to your great offense, how we are conducting ourselves, and you add such are the reports. But I can state to you that it is a lie, and if you want to listen to it, it will be your matter. I think those that live around here know best what kind of life we are living. I understand from your letter that our desire is to get rid of you. How can you talk this way? It has never entered my thoughts, but it has been yourself, and as the proverb says, 'As you make your bed, so will you lie.' You are yourself the cause of being where you are. Now consider the manner closely and imagine that we had a lot of boys instead of girls and that I had committed such a crime with our boys as you have with our girls; would you think well of it? I often spoke to you and cautioned you against such conduct, but you answered me that I should not bother myself about what you done with them. You remember well that you often said you would furnish money to leave, to give an opportunity to carry out your beastly deeds with your children, which is a blood shame. You have set them a bad example, your way of proceeding with the children that we in common have brought into this world, is inhuman, and what do you think of the responsibility? You remember well that I promised the children a punishment when they told me of it, and I could not believe that you were so low, but now it has been brought to light. Tell me if you can, all the times you took your shoes off and came in through the window to see if I had anyone with me, did you ever find anyone? It is time that our own children get an idea of this life you have carried on with them, so they can guard themselves against others. You cannot deny this, for I have both heard and seen it. You know I told you, you might leave and take everything and just leave me one cow and my children, so that there might be an end to such a life. They could not follow you to town, but you had to be naughty to them and they were afraid to stay at home alone with you and they cried when I talked of going anywhere, and when I spoke it, you busted out in madness. You have spent much to secure your freedom that you care not whether we have anything to eat or not. You might have gone this spring, and as they say around here, it was strange that you did not, when you were in such a shape, and as the report is 'there is more of it in Dakota.' I have enough to keep me in this wretched world; may you repent for your past life and finally obtain everlasting life. Dear Ole, when we entered the holy bond of matrimony, I did not think I should have to lead such a life with you. I have helped you as a wife but what have you done for us? You have put us down in the eyes of the people.

Farewell, Martha Narkin

Narkin was taken to Stillwater State Prison where he served out his sentence, three years and six months. Ole was discharged from the penitentiary on November 12, 1888.

But the story does not end here. It appeared Martha Narkin was no saint.

After Narkin was released from prison, he traveled home to reunite with his wife and children. He was excited to see his family again but when he arrived home, he found the house empty. He contacted neighbors and found out Martha and the children left sometime in the fall of 1888. Martha and the children secretly left the area to prevent Ole and the neighbors from finding out where they went.

Narkin filed for divorce on September 13, 1889. Since the court could not locate Martha, a public summons was placed in the *Granite Falls Tribune* for six consecutive weeks, beginning April 13 and ending on May 20, 1890.

The divorce hearing took place on December 2, 1890 in front of referee Ole Hartwick. Three witnesses were subpoenaed for the plaintiff, Ole Narkin. They were Edward Hanson, Charles Gunderson, and Carrie Narkin. Ole Narkin was the first sworn to testify. He stated he lived in Wergeland Township for fourteen years, was forty-nine years old, and his wife was fifty-one years old. Ole testified that on October 18, 1883, his wife, Martha, committed adultery and had illicit sexual intercourse with Charles (or Carl) Gunderson. In 1887 and 1888, Martha had illicit sexual intercourse with Charles Gunderson and for the last eight years Martha had a connection with this man. Ole said that he knew this to be true from the fact that after he had learned this from others, he asked Martha if she had sexual intercourse with Gunderson and she admitted that she had. This act of adultery took place while Ole was absent from home, in Dakota threshing. In the month of April 1885, Narkin went away from home and was continuously absent until the fall of 1888. This was during the time Ole spent in prison for incest.

"When I returned, I found Martha was gone and never was able to find her. I once heard that she had gone to Washington State. During my absence, I learned that Martha had committed adultery with different persons, that my home had been used as a house of ill fame, and was commonly called a 'whorehouse,' and Martha was called a 'whore.' I never lived or cohabited with Martha after I learned of the acts of adultery."

Edward Hanson testified he knew the Narkins for about seven years and worked for Ole in the past. While working for Ole one day, "I asked Martha if the stories about her and Charles Gunderson being intimate were true, and she admitted they were. I also asked Gunderson about these stories, and he said they were only stories and laughed. I saw Gunderson at Narkin's place one night and he was in the bedroom alone with Martha for a long time. When he came out, he was accused of having criminal connection with Martha, but he denied it, saying he had been in there mixing drinks."

Charles Gunderson was duly sworn and stated he knew the Narkins for about thirteen years and lived about ½ mile from their place. "I was twenty-nine years old, married, and had two children while I was involved with Martha. In the fall of 1888, Martha left the country, and I have not seen her since then. I knew of a good many people who went to Martha's house in the night and stayed there all night. The house had a very bad reputation and was commonly called a 'whorehouse.' They were mostly young men that went there, and all this occurred in the absence of Ole. A great many men told me they went to Narkin's house, stayed all night, and had illicit sexual intercourse with Martha."

Last to testify was Carrie Narkin, daughter of Ole and Martha. "I have heard about a certain trip my mother made with Gunderson from home to Canby and back. I asked my mother whether the story about her and Gunderson having sexual intercourse on that trip was true, to which she gave no answer. Gunderson used to visit our house quite often. He used to be alone in the house with my mother at times when my sister and I were going out. Gunderson tried on several occasions to have sexual intercourse with me. I left home at the beginning of 1886 and returned in the fall of the same year. I remained home about four weeks and then left again. During my absences, I received letters from home written by my sisters, who wrote that they were having good times and that lots of boys used to come there and they had dances. I have also heard that our home wore a bad reputation during this period."

On April 1, 1891, District Judge, C.S. Brown decreed that "the marriage between Ole and Martha Narkin be dissolved, and said parties were released from the bonds of matrimony and all obligations thereof." After the divorce, Narkin continued living in Granite Falls. He worked odd jobs and lived alone. He passed away from heart failure on August 20, 1910 and was buried in the Granite Falls City Cemetery. The whereabouts of Martha and what became of the children remains a mystery.

Ole Narkin's Monument
Granite Falls City Cemetery
(photo by author)

FIRECRACKER STARTS
AN INFERNO

AT ABOUT 4:00 on the morning of July 5, 1889, Granite Falls residents were awakened by the sound of the fire bell. Excited citizens rushed outside to see what caused the siren to go off. "It's on the east side," someone shouted, and looking in that direction, one could see the billows of smoke and fire in the air. Groups of men, women, and children were seen battling the flames, which by this time were quite widespread. The fire was first discovered in the blacksmith shop of Thomas O'Donnell near the downtown area. Eugene Brown was the first to discover it and made every effort to gain entrance to the building, but it was locked. Others came to his aid, and they forced the door open. They managed to retrieve some of the tools, but the heavy iron items could not be removed from the building in time.

By this time the fire engine had arrived and finding an old well near the Pillsbury elevator, water was obtained, and a stream thrown on the adjoining buildings. Several homes were so ravaged by the flames that they could not be saved. The men worked bravely and stood before the fierce heat to fight the raging monster. As they gained on the fire, it became evident that it would stop, if the wind did not rise to excite its fury.

The homeless people wandered around looking for articles that might be saved from the disaster. Mr. Blomgren's house was occupied by three families who all lost furniture and clothing. The insurance was $800, and the loss reached nearly twice that sum. His barn was filled with hay and feed and went up with the rest. Buildings across the street, including the large hotel and barn of S. Anderson were in peril, but by active work, they were saved. The small houses just north of the barn were saved by the application of wet blankets and water brought by the heroic women who assisted those in need.

As the sun rose on the scene, a sad picture presented itself. Perhaps two hundred people had gathered to witness the sight. Women looked for various keepsakes that might be saved from the ashes. One lady hunted for her pocketbook, which she found in the hands of a small child. Another woman searched for some silverware that had been taken out and carelessly dropped on the ground.

There were many different opinions as to the cause of the fire, but it's quite possible a firecracker that failed to explode properly, landed on the roof of the blacksmith shop sometime during the night, and by continual burning caught the shingles and fanned by a gentle breeze, ignited the wood, which gradually escalated into a raging inferno. This version is probably the correct one, although others claim a felony of arson was committed by a tramp. Those burned out did not know if they would rebuild, and all had the sympathy of the community in their misfortune.

Main Street in Granite Falls, c. 1880s
(photo from Yellow Medicine County Historical Society collection)

CRIME and CALAMITY

FATHER KILLS HIS SON

A FOUL AND unnatural murder was committed in the forenoon on October 31, 1893 in Burton township. The killing involved the close relationship of father and son. The parties involved in this case were Anton Baierl, age fifty-nine, a German immigrant, and his son, Joseph, age thirty-four. Anton Baierl was a farmer residing in the county for fourteen years. Before coming to this country, he served in the Prussian army and obtained the rank of corporal. Anton was a widower; his wife had passed away in 1871. Anton was held in high esteem by all those who knew him. He held the office of town treasurer of Burton township for five years. Joseph was a farmer, married, and father of five children. He was also the town clerk of Burton township.

Anton was immediately arrested by constable Henry King and placed in the county jail in Granite Falls. The following morning, a local reporter stopped at the jail to interview Anton. When asked if he had anything to say for publication, Anton stood before the open grating of his cell and was at first disposed to say nothing. He appeared quiet and calm, showing nothing to indicate brutality or the disposition to harm others in any way. Finally, he acknowledged that he shot

Joseph, and his story appeared in the *Reform Advocate*, November 1, 1893.

"There never was any trouble between Joseph and me until a year ago. Before then we were always on good terms. I have done everything I could for him. But a year ago, he turned against me."

"Why did he turn against you?" asked the reporter.

"I don't know, I can't tell. He calls me a thief—I don't know why. Yesterday morning I went to his place to get a harness belonging to me, to lend to my son-in-law. When I got there, they were stacking hay and Joseph came at me with a pitchfork. I told him to keep off, but he rushed nearer to me and I shot him."

"Did you intend to kill Joseph?"

"No! I don't quarrel with anybody—my neighbors will tell you so," and here the old man showed the only sign of emotion.

"Have you at any time since the shooting said that you were glad you had killed Joseph?" "No, I never said that," Anton replied.

The trial would, without a doubt, show that the quarrel had its origin in some question of property. It was reported on the streets that this was the case and that there was a long-standing feud between the two men about some land.

Anton Baierl was given a preliminary examination on November 10, before Justice James Putnam, who held court in the engine house. County Attorney Ole Hartwick prosecuted the case, and Attorney Andrew Volstead appeared for the defense. The examination occupied the entire day, and it was 9 p.m. before it was completed. The State endeavored to show that the deed was premeditated and that the old man went to Joseph's place with murder in his heart and that he lost no time in putting his thoughts into action when he arrived. The defense did not put any witnesses on the stand, preferring not to show their line of defense at this time, but it would undoubtedly be that the old man killed his son in self-defense. The defendant was denied bail and remanded to the county jail to await the action of the grand jury.

While Baierl was confined in his tiny, dark prison cell, he became very despondent, ever since Attorney Volstead decided not to defend him; instead, Attorney Schellbach took the case. On January 4, 1894, Baierl attempted to kill himself by opening an artery in his left arm, from which he came near to bleeding to death. He had somehow managed to retain possession of a teaspoon and had sharpened the end of the handle so that he was able to sever an artery in his arm. He took the precaution to lay a quilt on the floor so that the man in the next cell could not hear the drip of the blood. The only thing that saved him was the fact that he fainted from the loss of blood and when he did so, the blood stopped flowing. Had he reopened the wound when he came to, he would soon have been dead, but he did not do this. At about 1 a.m., he called out "goodbye" to the man in the next cell, and the man heard him, but paid no attention to it. Baierl's cell presented a very bloody appearance in the morning.

At one point, Baierl tried to borrow a jackknife from Sheriff Jensvold on the pretense of desiring to cut his fingernails, but the sheriff refused to let him have it, and said he was certain that had he let him have the knife, he would have then attempted to kill himself. Now Baierl said he would not attempt self-destruction again but would wait for someone else to do it for him. The sheriff made sure he was watched from then on.

Before the trial, defense Attorney Volstead requested a "change of venue." Because of the townspeople's hostile feeling toward Baierl, newspaper publicity, and neighborhood gossip, Volstead felt the defendant would not get a fair trial. But Attorney Ole Hartwick felt there were a number of people residing in the county that were suitable to sit as jurors, who were not biased nor prejudiced against the defendant, who had not made up their mind as to the guilt or innocence of the defendant, and who did not know the particulars of the crime nor under what circumstances the crime was committed, and so a "change of venue" was denied.

The judge set a special term of court for February 27, 1894. The case was opened by County Attorney Hartwick, who told the jury all about the case and just what the prosecution expected to be able to prove. The first witness called was Susan Baierl. Her testimony was the same as in the preliminary examination. She stated that Anton had brought back the drag and took back the harness and told Joseph to bring the contract to church on Sunday. "Joe agreed to give up the contract, there was no quarrel over that. Joe had a pitchfork in his hands with the tines sticking in the ground. Joe was not mad and showed no madness at all toward his father. I never witnessed any difficulty between Joe and his father. They had a quarrel in November 1892 about some corn, but that did not amount to much. They made a contract for the place after that. Anton did plowing during the summer and helped in the work, but there was no difficulty about the division of the crop. I am not mad at Anton now. It wouldn't do me any good if I was."

John Hay was sworn in and testified that he went with Constable King to arrest Baierl at Rader's place at about 11 a.m.

Another witness called was John Knight. He stated he had a conversation with Baierl on the seventh day of June at a town board meeting. It was about the defendant's office as treasurer and his circumstances and state of feeling. Anton said his son had taken all the property he had and now he had to work for a living. Joseph was there at the meeting. A complaint was made to have him (Anton) removed from office because of his being a non-resident. Anton said that a boy who would use his father the way Joe did ought to be shot like a dog.

Dr. A.R. Torgerson was called to testify. He stated that he was a physician and surgeon. "On November 1, 1893, I was called to visit Joseph Baierl. I did not hold an autopsy but held an inquest. This was three miles west of St. Leo. I found a bullet wound one inch in front of the ear on the left side. I used the sound and the probe. I traced the course of the bullet and determined that it lay on the base of the skull. A great deal of bleeding would naturally result. The hole was oblong, up and down; there were gunpowder marks near the wound. I did not find the bullet; the bullet did not come out of the head but lay at the base of the brain at the back of the right ear."

CRIME and CALAMITY

The State rested its case. The opening argument for the defendant was made by attorney L.H. Schellbach. He outlined the evidence that would be introduced. The revolver was introduced into evidence and admitted by the defendant to be the instrument used.

The defendant, Anton Baierl, was called to the stand to testify on his own behalf. He stated he went to his son's place about 9:30 that morning. "I wanted to take a harrow back and get an ox harness, also wanted to get my contract. I drove to where they were hauling hay, drove back of his wagon about five or six feet. Joe was on the north side of the wagon near the front wheel. His wife was in front of the oxen. I told him that was my plow, and he was a thief. He said, 'That is enough, I am just as good a man as you are, you had better try to get off.' Then he came for me with a pitchfork. I told him to keep back or I would shoot, but he came close to me. I did not take aim, did not have time, he came so quick. He had the fork in both hands and looked mad. I could not get out of the box so quick. Just as the bullet struck him, he jumped back, turned, and fell. I was so scared, I did not know what to do; then she came at me with the fork over her head and I told her to keep away or I have some left to shoot. Then I drove home and got my town book and entered in order in the records."

"From there I went to William Rader's. I went into the cellar to get something to eat before I started for Canby. When Rader told me that Hay wanted me, I came right out of the cellar. I explained to them how it was that he came for me with the fork. I bought the revolver in Marshall in April, as I lived alone after Joe had moved away from my place. It was in my pocket the morning I went to Joe's place. He had agreed to give the contract up in June; there was no trouble about that. I told my son in the spring of 1892 that I would give him the farm. I was present at the town meeting; the trouble referred to was, that a complaint was made that I was not a resident, I was not removed. I used harsh words there but only to reprimand Joe. I do not know who made the complaint. There was no hard feeling between me and Joe. He came up within three feet of me and I told him to keep back or I would show him something, but he came right on. I fired the gun. I just thought I would scare him back, then his wife came for me. I did not point the gun at her, I had it in my hand. The gun was about three feet from Joe when the shot was fired. He was so close to me that I thought the tines were against my side. There was not much time to think, all was done so quickly."

William Rader was a witness for the defense. He stated that he had just come from the field when Baierl drove up. "He told me how it came that he shot Joe. He said he and Joe had a quarrel and that Joe came at him with a fork, and he told Joe to keep back, and had to shoot to keep him off or he would have struck him. The defendant said he was going to Canby to tell the justice just how the thing was and give himself up. I knew Joe, he was not quick-tempered but was very high-tempered."

Mary Rader testified stating she was the wife of William Rader and a daughter of the defendant. "I was at home October 31 and saw nothing strange about my father that morning. Joe was my brother. I knew his disposition. He was not quick-tempered but high-tempered. When he was mad, he was very mad."

The State and defense rested their case. Judge Powers charged the jury and the case was given into their hands. They came to an agreement and returned a verdict of manslaughter in the first degree. The judge announced he would pass sentence at 3 p.m., and court adjourned until that time. That afternoon, the courtroom was packed with men and women to hear the sentence and listen to what the counsel on either side, or the judge had to say about the case and the sentence. Judge Powers sentenced the prisoner to a term of six years at hard labor in the state prison at Stillwater. The sentence was hailed with delight by the prisoner, who expected to receive a much longer sentence. In fact, he expected no other fate than that of being hanged. With this light of a sentence, he would undoubtedly serve less than five years behind bars.

The general sentiment among the people appeared to be that he should have had at least ten years, and this would have pleased most everyone. The people living in the town of Burton and that part of the county were very bitter over the outcome of the trial. It was a well-known fact that had Baierl not been taken out of town as soon as he was after the murder, he would have been lynched the same day. The old man seemed to have a bad reputation. Attorneys Schellbach and Volstead were certainly to be congratulated for the way they conducted the defense. The prisoner hugged them, expressing a deep appreciation for their efforts on his behalf.

Baierl was transported to the Stillwater State Prison by Sheriff Jensvold. He adjusted well to prison life and was a model inmate, obeying all the laws of the prison system. The warden kept a close watch on Baierl as he had heard about the suicide attempt. In June 1898 the parole board reviewed Baierl's case. At that time, it was determined the prisoner had served enough time for his crime. He was released from the Stillwater State Prison on June 23, 1898, serving four years of a six-year sentence. He moved back to his farm.

At some point, he gave up the farm and moved in with his daughter, Mary Rader. He lived with her for sixteen years and was well taken care of. He passed away at home on May 15, 1927. He was ninety-two years old at the time of his death and was buried in the St. Leo Catholic cemetery.

Was justice served in this case? Was "old man Baierl" insane, as many people claimed, or did he merely act in self-defense? Would a "change of venue" have made a difference in the outcome of this trial? Whatever the case, it was clearly shown in the minds of most people that the old man went to the son's place for a purpose which he accomplished when the fatal shot was fired and that five children and a heart-stricken wife demanded that speedy justice be served to a red-handed slayer of a father and a husband.

Sketch of Anton Baierl
(from Granite Falls Journal, March 8, 1894)

Anton Baierl's Marker
St. Leo Catholic Cemetery, St. Leo, MN
(photo from "Find a Grave")

CRIME and CALAMITY

A STABBING AFFAIR

A BAD STABBING occurred on the night of September 17, 1896, about 8 miles east of Canby when a quarrel broke out between Thomas Nelson and Harry DeVere. Earlier that day the two men had been threshing at Charles Voss' farm without incident. After work, they went into town for some refreshments and came back to the farm with half a keg of beer. According to witnesses, Tom and Harry exchanged unsavory words after supper, and Tom pushed Harry to the ground. The two men drank some alcohol before supper and commenced drinking beer about 7 p.m. Around 8 p.m. they went to the barn to get ready for bed, as their sleeping quarters were in the hayloft. August Voss said that Tom was standing on one side and Harry on the other, between the horses, and Harry told Tom to get up and they would go to bed, and Tom said he did not feel like it, so Tom hauled off and hit Harry in the face, and afterwards they both started in. They were standing and then dropped down between the horses.

Farmhands, George Maxfield and Jim Cleary, who were in the hayloft at the time, heard the commotion, came downstairs, and parted the two men. Tom was on top of Harry, and Tom immediately said,

"Hurry up and get the doctor." George picked up Tom and carried him out of the barn. Harry told the boys, "I have stabbed him good and deep. I am sorry, but I could not help it. Tom forced it on me."

Dr. James McPeek, the Canby physician, came to the Voss farm later that evening to administer aid to Tom. He had several wounds which were probably caused by a sharp instrument, possibly a knife. One wound was directly over the left eye, extending downward and across the bridge of the nose and cut to the bone. The wound on the right side, at about the junction of the fourth rib, was cut to the bone. There was a puncture wound on the left chest. There was another wound on the left side between the ninth and tenth rib, about midway between the sternum and spine. The doctor dressed the wounds and came out the following day. He noticed that Tom's fever had come up considerably and he was in a dangerous condition. The second day after the incident, Tom died.

The coroner's inquest was held on September 19, with the post mortem examination performed by Coroner Torgerson and Dr. McPeek. It was determined that Nelson died from hemorrhage and inflammation of the lungs from the wound in his chest which was inflicted by a sharp instrument penetrating the lung and pleural cavity, causing his death. It was never clearly determined what the argument was about, but liquor may have played a big part in this tragic incident.

A warrant was issued for the arrest of Harry DeVere on September 22. Sheriff Borre Peterson went out and brought in the man and placed him in the county jail. The prisoner denied any knowledge of the affair and stoutly proclaimed his innocence. But a knife covered with blood was found on his person, and there was one man who saw the fight. The evidence was strong against the prisoner. The grand jury indicted Harry DeVere for the crime of "murder in the first degree" on January 12, 1897. The offence was not bailable, and the defendant was placed in the county jail to await his trial.

At the trial on January 20, 1897, County Attorney Andrew Volstead appeared for the State, and Attorney Ole Ostensoe represented the defendant. The prosecution laid out all the evidence and August Voss, the eyewitness, explained in detail what he saw, so there was no doubt about what happened that night. The defense did not have a strong case, and no character witnesses were called to testify in Harry's defense. It appears DeVere did not have a chance of a light sentence. The jury found Harry DeVere guilty of murder in the second degree which was a lesser charge then was found in the indictment.

Before sentencing, Harry spoke before the judge that he was once an iron worker in Pittsburg. Since then he had rambled here and there having no real home. He had no other trade or profession and had worked as a farm laborer during harvesting and threshing. He had never been convicted of any crime. The judge sentenced DeVere to a life of hard labor at Stillwater State Prison. He took his sentence calmly and never exhibited a noticeable regret as the words that sealed his destiny were spoken.

This seems like a very harsh punishment for this offense, when it's clear that Nelson struck DeVere with his fist and felled him, after which the stabbing affair occurred in the barn. And so, a little whiskey, some bitter language, and the brutal stabbing cost Nelson his life and DeVere his liberty for the rest of his natural life. It's quite possible Harry was afraid of Tom after the altercation that occurred earlier that day and acted in self-defense. In this instance, both men had consumed much alcohol, and things got out of control. At the trial, August Voss gave conflicting comments in his testimony. George Maxfield failed to appear in court to give his testimony, and no character witnesses testified in Harry's defense. Attorney Ole Ostensoe presented a poor defense for his client, resulting in a blatant miscarriage of justice. This clearly appeared to be a case of self-defense in which the defendant should have been accquitted, but instead, Harry, spent the rest of his life behind bars.

A DRUNKEN BRAWL

AUSTIN AND MARTIN Olson were brothers who were good friends when sober, but bitter enmity existed between them when they were intoxicated. The two men lived about a mile apart, just a few miles west of Canby. Martin was single and lived with his mother. Austin had a wife and family who left him because of his brutal treatment of them when he was intoxicated. Both men were drunkards. Martin was the one that usually obtained the liquor and brought it to Austin's home. The men started out on a cordial note, but after copious amounts of alcohol were consumed, fierce brawls broke out. The brothers drank until they were so drunk and exhausted they could not move. Martin was always the aggressor in these drunken bouts and had a quarrelsome disposition. Austin, on the other hand, was usually a very law-abiding citizen, except when drunk, he could get vicious.

On Saturday or Sunday, January 2 or 3, 1897, Martin went to the home of his brother, taking with him a jug of whiskey, and they lost no time in disposing of it between them. Once this was consumed, Martin went to Canby to get more liquor and returned with another half-gallon of alcohol. The two brothers remained alone in Austin's shanty, continued to drink, and became very intoxicated. Austin's shanty was a small, one-room building, containing a bed, cook stove, some furniture, tools, and numerous wooden boxes.

In the early part of the evening, the two brothers, who were nearly matched in physical strength, danced, wrestled, and fought with each other, both becoming severely bruised and battered. Austin finally became tired and lay down on his bed to sleep, but Martin kept up the dancing and drinking for quite some time. Austin fell asleep and was awakened by a rattling noise near the stove in the room and saw Martin standing over him, striking at his head, saying, "I have got you now and will finish you up." Austin stated that he was struck in the head by some instrument and knew nothing more of what happened.

The following morning, when Austin awoke, he called to Martin repeatedly to bring him some water. He received no answer, so he crawled out of bed and found Martin lying in the middle of the floor. Austin called out to him again and felt his arm, but it was cold and stiff. Austin was in a daze, his head throbbed, and he noticed his clothes were spattered with blood. He knew Martin was in trouble and needed medical attention. Austin put on his winter coat and boots, stepped outside into a snowstorm and partly crawled and walked to his neighbor's, Ole Jorgenson, about 3/4 of a mile down the road, through deep snow, in a horrible blizzard. He arrived at Jorgenson's house about noon, and asked him to check on Martin, who he thought was dead. Austin looked more dead than alive when he arrived at Jorgenson's place. His face and head were badly cut and bruised, his hair and beard matted, and shirt and clothing saturated in blood. The snow was so deep and the storm so bad that it was impossible for Jorgenson to go for help until the following day. When the weather cleared, Jorgenson went to the neighbors and together, they traveled to Austin's place where they found Martin dead on the floor in a pool of blood with many scalp wounds that appeared to have been made with some instrument like an iron rod or iron tongs. Lying on the floor, near Martin, was a pair of tongs commonly used by blacksmiths and somewhat stained with blood. The pillow and bed where Austin slept the night before was also saturated with blood. Austin always maintained that he did not know anything about how his brother was killed, and that he did not remember anything after being struck in the head by Martin.

The wounds on Martin's head were numerous, twelve or more, including some on the face and others on the left side and back of the head. Dr. James McPeek examined the body and noticed the skull was fractured in two places, one over the left eye, the other above the left temple. These wounds would have caused Martin's death.

The bed had the appearance of being used by only one person. Between the bed and the stove there were some blankets, doubled up as though used for a pillow. These blankets were saturated with blood, and there was blood spattered on the walls near the blankets.

It was shown by the physician called to attend to Austin a day or two after this tragedy that Austin was badly injured too. He had been severely struck on the head and other parts of the body, and from these injuries he appeared very depressed and confused mentally. He was so lame that he could hardly walk and had many bruises on his face and head.

The doctor commented that when a person receives a severe blow on the head, unconsciousness is a probable consequence, and that while unconscious, he may continue a fight in which he is engaged without knowing what he is doing, and that when he recovers consciousness, he will have no recollection whatsoever of what took place in his unconscious state.

Austin's story was that Martin pounded him nearly to death and then committed suicide, but his story was not credible. Evidence and circumstances pointed to his connection with the fearful tragedy. A pair of iron tongs and a stick of wood lay on the floor not far from the dead man's body. The floor and bed were spattered with blood and gave evidence that a terrible encounter had taken place. Austin Olson was arrested and placed in the county jail. He would await the action of the grand jury. A few weeks later, the jury brought in an indictment of "manslaughter in the first degree." Olson would await his trial in March of that year.

After the trial, on March 22, 1897, the jury brought in the verdict "guilty of manslaughter in the first degree." Austin Olson was sentenced to eight years at Stillwater State Prison. He was sixty-two years old.

About three years later, on January 8, 1900, Austin's sentence was commuted by the Board of Pardons to five years, and he walked out of prison a free man. A petition had been filed by citizens and business merchants of Canby, the trial judge and county attorney, and eleven of the jurors who once convicted him, stating that in view of all the facts and circumstances revealed at the trial, Austin had suffered sufficient punishment, and the degree of the crime was higher than the evidence warranted. Time had wrought quite a change in Austin's appearance. His hair had turned from black to quite gray, he was clean-shaven, and his skin appeared white from the long confinement behind bars. Now all he had to do was continue the reform that prison life had required of him, and the remainder of his days could be spent in usefulness. He was getting well along in years and confinement in prison had taken its toll.

The sentence might have seemed rather light for the offence committed, but there were, no doubt, extenuating circumstances. Both men were evidently drunk the night of the tragedy, and engaged in a fight, as the prisoner plainly showed when arrested, and of course, there was the possibility that Austin may have killed his brother in self-defense.

This was clearly a case of two brothers consuming too much alcohol, with one ending up dead. Austin was a quiet man and had the best of records in prison. He was just a poor, old farmer who truly loved his brother, and never would intentionally harm him in any way. Austin's only crime was being the victim of too much strong drink. The crime was the result of a terrible drunken brawl between two brothers, rather than because of any criminal intent or knowledge on the part of Austin Olson. If it had not been for the great amount of liquor consumed by the brothers, there probably never would have been a homicide in this case.

DEATH IN A BURNING BARN

A SHAPELESS MASS of charred bones was all that was left to tell the story of one of the most fatal catastrophes that ever occurred in this county—four unknown persons lost their lives. It happened about 3 a.m. on October 14, 1897, just four miles southwest of Hanley Falls. Sivert Berg just happened to discover his barn on fire. The blaze had made some headway before it was noticed, and all efforts to save the building were fruitless. It was destroyed, along with 100 tons of hay, 1900 bushels of grain, and 10 horses.

The ruins of the barn burned for two or three days, and it was impossible to begin removing the debris until the fire was extinguished. A group of men were at the scene sifting through the smoldering embers. It wasn't long before one of the men discovered the charred remains of a human being. The men immediately set to work to find out if there were any more victims, and by nightfall, they had unearthed three more bodies. The bodies were almost entirely cremated and when they tried to move them, the bones disintegrated so it was impossible to identify them as being those of humans.

Coroner Dr. Donnell from Clarkfield viewed the remains and

decided not to hold an inquest, as there were no suspicious circumstances connected with the affair. The most plausible theory given for the cause of the fire and the fatalities of the men, was that they had crawled up into the hayloft for a night's rest and probably fell asleep while one or more of them were smoking. Then a hot ember from a pipe or cigarette ignited the hay. However, this was only a theory and the cause of the fire, as well as, the identity of the men who perished in the flames, would forever remain a mystery. Mr. Berg's personal loss on the barn and contents was $3,500; insurance covered $1,700.

Another article appeared in the newspaper the following week. People in the area wanted to know the identity of the men who perished in the fire. An obvious theory was that they were tramps and settled for the night in Berg's barn. But rumors later came in that a handkerchief was found with several pieces of iron tied in one corner and that two of the best horses owned by Mr. Berg were missing. This complicated the tragedy and gave a suspicion that murder may have been committed, along with arson. Nothing more was reported in the newspapers following this tragedy and no further investigation was implemented at the time. Was the fire started by a hot ember from a pipe or cigarette, or was the fire an act of arson to coverup the possible murder of four men who were found trespassing on private property, or did Sivert Berg set fire to his barn to collect insurance money to pay his many debts? No one knows for sure what happened, except that four innocent men lost their lives that night.

BEATEN WITH A BILLY

JOSEPH OTT OF Echo Township murdered his wife in cold blood on the evening of May 18, 1898. Ott was forty-three years old, of German and Jewish descent, and came to the county from Sleepy Eye in 1888, settling on farm four miles south of Echo. He married Louise Dohrmann, daughter of Henry and Caroline Dohrmann of Sleepy Eye, Brown County, on February 28, 1878. The marriage was a big mistake right from the start and a most unhappy one. Ever since the birth of their first child, Ott had been brutal and cruel. When his wife presented him with their first-born son, Ott said, "I wished the baby was dead and we parted." This gives a key note into their married life. They had six children, the oldest being nineteen years of age and the youngest, a boy of three years.

Ott was an abusive husband and a tyrant in his home, flying into a heated rage at the least provocation and venting his anger in assaults on his wife and children. Ott took real pleasure in inflicting pain on a dumb animal or on a human being. As an example of his ungovernable temper, he once took his knife and dug out one eye of a bull because the animal would not go into the stable when he wanted it to. A few days later, he again tried to make the bull go into the stable and because it was stubborn and would not, he dug out the other eye. For this horrendous deed, his neighbors had him arrested.

On June 15, 1886, Ott beat and pounded his oldest son, Samuel, so brutally and seriously that the neighbors intervened. His wife attempted to shield the boy, but she was kicked out of the house. Samuel carried the scars from this brutal attack for the rest of his life and never forgave his father for trying to kill him. Ott had, time and again, brutally beaten his wife and driven her from the home on many occasions. He threatened not only to kill her, but also, her father and mother. Louise left Ott and commenced action for a divorce in March 1887. But pending the suit, they patched up their trouble. Joe promised to be a better husband and succeeded in persuading Louise to withdraw the petition, thus abandoning the suit.

On the day of the murder, Louise and Samuel attended a wedding in the neighborhood. They took all the children with them, leaving Ott at home alone. To pass the time, he read from the book *The Assassination of Garfield*. Toward evening, Mrs. Ott and her son returned home to help with chores, leaving the other children at a neighbor's house. Their intention was to return to the dance at the place where the marriage had taken place earlier that day. Ott was in the yard when Louise and Samuel drove up. Louise got out of the wagon and went into the house, followed by Ott. He was angry because they had been at the wedding and yelled at his wife as soon as she entered the house. He asked her where the children were, and she told him they were at the neighbor's because she and her son intended to return to the dance. Louise asked Ott to come along. He said he would not go and that she should not either. They continued their quarreling for a few more minutes when he struck her.

Ott told the following story of how he killed his wife, and always told it as one might tell of how one killed some wild animal. "She had been at the wedding and was going back and wanted me to go along. I did not want to go, and we got into some words. Then I struck her several times with my fist, but I saw I could not give her enough that way and went and got the billy. I struck her several times with this and told her I had been divorced from her once and now I would give her a divorce that would last. She said, 'Oh, Joe, don't kill me. Don't strike me anymore and I won't say any more about it.' Then I caught her by the hair and dragged her out of the bedroom and I'll bet I struck her fifteen times with the billy."

Ott then went out and told his son he had killed his mother. The son immediately started for Echo and on the way, stopped at the nearest neighbor, Charles Cooper's place, and told him what had happened. Cooper went at once to the Ott farm. He arrived at the residence and saw Ott pacing back and forth in front of the house. Cooper asked Ott if it was true that his wife was hurt. "Yes," said Ott, "and she's hurt pretty bad, too." Ott asked Cooper if he wanted to see her. Cooper accompanied Ott into the house and pointed to the body of his wife, who was writhing in the agonies of death. "There she is," said Ott. Cooper asked him what he hit her with, and Ott said, "This," holding up the bloody billy. The billy was one of those leather-covered ones loaded with shot or iron at one end. This weapon had been in the house some twenty years, Ott having purchased it in Chicago. Ott expressed no sorrow over having killed his wife an hour after the homicide occurred, saying, "I might as well be dead as living the cat and dog life I have been living." The following is a description of the crime scene as reported in the local newspaper.

The door between the kitchen and sitting room was shut but on the kitchen side of the door was a horrible pool of blood about three feet across. Ott opened the door. Louise was lying on the carpet, weltering in another pool of her own blood, while numerous spots of clotted blood, and what seemed to be brains were lying all

about her. She was not dead but was breathing heavily and mov-
ing about some as if in pain. The murderer held the light close to
her head and we saw that her eyes and face were pounded to a jelly
and that her forehead and side of the head were literally covered
with deep gashes from which slowly oozed her life blood. She had
then been lying there about two hours and she lived about another
half hour longer, finally dying at around 9 p.m.

Deputy Sheriff Milo Beard soon arrived from Echo and at once placed Ott under arrest and brought him to Granite Falls that same night. Had he been allowed to remain in Echo that night, he never would have lived to be hanged. There were strong threats of lynching, and for that reason, Sheriff Schwalier took extra precautions with his prisoner for quite some time.

Louise Ott's funeral took place at the German Methodist Church in Echo. Among those who attended the service were her mother and brother from Sleepy Eye, and her sister and brother-in-law from Lamberton. After the funeral, the remains were placed on the 12:35 train to Sleepy Eye. The deceased was interred in the Durbahn family plot in the Home Cemetery at Sleepy Eye. After Louise's death, Caroline Durbahn (Louise's sister) raised the children. The family did not want Louise buried next to the brutal man who murdered her, so she was buried in the Durbahn family plot without a headstone.

A preliminary examination took place, and Ott was held to await the action of the grand jury. The prisoner did not deny his guilt. The June term of court convened a few weeks after the terrible deed had been committed, and the trial of Ott was soon over. The grand jury found an indictment against him and he was at once taken before the court to plead. He pled guilty to the charge of murder. The court appointed two lawyers to defend him, because earlier he had declined the services of any lawyer. When the case was again called, Ott stood up and said he was guilty as charged. Judge Qvale sentenced him, "that after the expiration of three calendar months, on a day set by the governor, Joseph Ott was to be hung by the neck until he was dead."

Ott never flinched or made the least sign or movement to show his feelings. It simply did not affect him, and he turned and walked out of the room with the sheriff as though nothing unusual had happened. The fact was, he seemed perfectly willing to die. He took his sentence with the same degree of emotion any ordinary man might take a sentence of one day in jail. And from that time, he never seemed to care as to his fate. He had always said he killed his wife and was ready to die for it. Ott's children were at the trial, and he asked them if they would forgive him; the girls said they would, but Samuel said, "No, you killed my mother and tried to kill me, and I will not forgive you."

After Judge Qvale had passed sentence upon Ott and ordered him to be removed from the courtroom and taken to his cell in the jail, he told the bailiff to lock the door and let no one out until he gave them permission. The courtroom was crowded with people and all had to remain until the judge considered sufficient time had elapsed to allow the prisoner to reach the jail. This was done to prevent any attempted lynching mob.

The scaffold for the execution was built in the jail yard right up against the south end of the jail. Sheriff Joseph H. Schwalier was charged with the duty of carrying out the sentence. A seven-foot-high board stockade 36' x 60' was erected behind the jail within which the gallows were built so that no one on the outside could see what was going on, on the inside. Every detail for the execution was carefully carried out by Sheriff Schwalier, and nothing was left undone.

The governor set the date of execution for October 20, 1898. On the day before the scheduled hanging, Ott's six children came up from Echo and visited their father for the last time. At Ott's request, Sheriff Schwalier let the children into the cell where he sat with them on the cot. The scene was a very emotional one. Ott broke down and cried like a child, and of course, the children cried bitterly. Even the son, who had previously refused to forgive his father or have anything to do with him, broke down and cried. Ott informed his children that he had transferred all his property to them, and said, "It is only just and proper that I should do some good in this world before I am compelled to depart from it."

For many weeks, Ott appeared very calm and resigned to his fate, but as his days drew nearer to the execution, he showed unmistakable signs of weakening, and said he would rather do hard labor for life at Stillwater than hang. Since his confinement, he had found the Lord and repented for this terrible deed. Ott had a Lutheran minister with him daily. He read the Bible and prayed when not engaged in conversation with visitors.

On October 20, 1898, the day of the execution, the wind howled, rain pelted the ground, there was a cold nip in the air, and to make matters worse, a pasty mass of trampled mud was underfoot. Some four hundred men occupied the enclosure, and a large crowd stood outside where they could see the procession as it passed from the jail into the yard, but there was not a sound, nothing that would have told a blindfolded man he was in the presence of many people. Every hat came off when the procession started from the door to the yard. The jail yard was brightly lit with electric lights so that all could see plainly. It was a most solemn scene, and one no person present would ever forget. Ott selected witnesses for his execution, H.F. Dohrmann and A. Durbahn of Sleepy Eye and August Henachke of Echo.

If there were those who expected to see Ott break down at the last minute, they were mistaken. When the sheriff entered his cell at a few minutes past one o'clock and told him they were ready, Ott got up off the bed and stood erect while the death warrant was read to him as the law directed. His face was just a little pale, but that was all. He then helped put on the black mantle, putting it on as he might a coat. He then walked out of his jail cell into the cold, dark night. It was still raining, and Ott seemed comforted by the droplets landing upon his sad, weary face. The death march was led by Ott's three spiritual advisers, who walked to the extreme left of the scaffold. Next were his two brothers-in-law, then two members of the death watch.

Following these closely came the condemned man, guarded on either side by deputies, with Sheriff Schwalier bringing up the rear. With a firm step, Ott slowly walked around the building to the scaffold and up thirteen steep, narrow steps to the top of the landing. The condemned man stood erect on the trap-door, with the two deputies retaining their hold on him and sustaining him when he showed signs of tottering, which he did twice.

It was 1:17 a.m. when the prisoner ascended the steps to the gallows. His spiritual advisors read from the scriptures, and Rev. Fjeldsted read a chapter from the Bible in English, followed by a prayer in German by Rev. Rabe. When asked if he had anything to say, Ott slowly raised his head and cast his eyes over the large crowd in front of him and said in substance, "Friends, I am sorry for what I did to my wife, and I want you to pray for me. If I had read my Bible and loved the Lord as I should have done, I would not have done what I did. But the devil was behind me. Dear friends, trust in the Lord, and you will never face the shame that I have tonight. Dear friends, I bid you good night."

Deputy Beard pulled the black cap down over the face of the doomed man, the noose was placed around his neck, and the arms and legs were quickly pinioned. The ministers began repeating the Lord's Prayer in unison and when they reached, "Thy will be done," Sheriff Schwalier pulled the lever, the drop fell, the body shot downward with a quick jolt, and the soul of Joseph Ott passed into eternity. The time was 1:23, he was pronounced dead at 1:28 by the physician, cut down at 1:30 and turned over to the undertaker. The neck was broken and the rope, 7/16 of an inch in size, cut into the flesh on the front part of the neck to sever the windpipe and jugular vein. Death was instantaneous, and the victim never moved a muscle after the drop. There was not a hitch anywhere in the proceedings. An execution could not have been more successful. Everyone present was in tears, moved by the affecting scene.

CRIME and CALAMITY

As one might imagine, there was a group of boys that wanted to witness the hanging and planned on being present when Joe stepped off into eternity. While they realized they could not get inside the high board fence, there were two large trees at the edge of the fence that the boys depended on for a seat and a grandstand view. The boys slept in Viken's barn that night and set the alarm on an old clock to awaken them in time to witness the hanging. And as fate would have it, the alarm did not go off. When the boys finally awoke, they hurried out the barn and ran up the dark alley to see the excitement, only to find that the hanging had already occurred. By the time the boys got to the jail, the crowd had dispersed. Ott's body had just been cut down and was laid out on a green window shutter alongside the fence. People gathered around it. The boys wanted to show their elders how brave they were, so they elbowed their way into the front rank. As they stood looking down at the dead man, there was a crack of lighting and a peal of thunder, everyone jumped. The boys immediately started for home, but they didn't go down the dark alley; instead, they went around the front of the jail and ran as fast as they could to their homes. These boys must have had a tough time falling asleep that night.

This marked the closing chapter in the life of Joseph Ott. Justice was finally meted out to the man who coolly pounded his wife to death while she begged for mercy. Joseph Ott's funeral was held in Granite Falls the following day, with Rev. Rabe conducting the service. His remains were not claimed by relatives or friends, so he was buried in an unmarked grave in Potters' Field east of Granite Falls. The Ott execution was the only one performed in the county. Sheriff Schwalier was awarded $350 for the execution of Ott, out of which he had to pay about $50 in expenses. The rope used was cut into short pieces and passed out to witnesses as souvenirs.

Joseph Ott   Executioner Sheriff Schwalier
(photos from Granite Falls Tribune, October 25, 1898)

Joseph Schwalier was a prosperous farmer of Canby and after retiring as sheriff, he was called upon to aid and assist sheriffs throughout the state whenever they needed help with an execution. He became known as an "official hangman" but was not proud of his experience as an executioner. Schwalier witnessed four legal executions in the State of Minnesota. At one of these, it was he who sent a brutal murderer into eternity, and at the other three, he helped to arrange all the details.

Schwalier witnessed the hanging of John Moshik in the Hennepin County Jail in March 1898, at which time he was one of the visiting and assisting sheriffs. In March 1901, Schwalier was present at the hanging of Fred Waller at Henderson, and had it not been for his

       CRIME and CALAMITY

experience in such matters, Sheriff Gaffke would have made a sorry spectacle of the affair. Schwalier furnished the ropes, made suggestions regarding the scaffold, which he helped build, and assisted the sheriff with all the arrangements.

When Sheriff August Johnson of Chaska was delegated to hang Andrew Tapper in February 1902, the sheriff immediately sent for Schwalier to assist him. Schwalier took almost the entire charge of the arrangements and everything went well. Some of those present at the execution thought Johnson failed at the last moment to pull the lever, and Schwalier had done the hanging. But this was vigorously denied by both Sheriff Johnson and his assistants. Joseph Schwalier will always be credited with hanging more people than any other man in Minnesota. Schwalier had in his possession several gruesome relics that he kept from each execution. These included pieces of rope, death shrouds, and even the "bloody billy" with which Ott killed his wife.

Later, Schwalier got involved in the hotel business. In 1908, he took possession of the American House in Little Falls, MN. He was a fine gentleman and furnished the best accommodations to his patrons. The hotel had all the modern conveniences, including steam heat and baths. It was well furnished, clean, comfortable, and service was first-class in all respects. The splendid meals furnished were a distinct attraction for travelers. Room rates were $1.00 or $1.25 per day. Schwalier was known to go after board-bill-jumpers. He followed one man to the local depot and demanded he pay his bill or suffer the consequences. The first boarder who attempted to jump his board bill, since Schwalier took charge of the hotel, was caught and spent thirty days in jail. After that episode, the man never jumped another board bill ever again.

Louise Ott buried in Durbahn family plot without a headstone
Home Cemetery in Sleepy Eye
(photo by author)

CRIME and CALAMITY

POISON AND A PAIR
OF SCISSORS

THE SETTLEMENT OF Friendship township, in which Clarkfield is situated, was begun in 1872, but there was no thought of founding a village until the Minneapolis & St. Louis Railroad pushed its way northwest through the county in 1884. Track-layers reached the site of the town in August, and in November of that year, regular train service was established. Clarkfield was platted October 7, 1884, by Charles F. Hatch, trustee. The original plat contained land on the northwest quarter of section 9 and consisted of twenty-seven blocks laid out on both sides of the railroad. Lots were placed on sale and the town of Clarkfield was founded. Clarkfield was named for a Mr. Clark, a railroad agent, and was incorporated in 1887.

Few circumstances are known surrounding the tragedy of County Coroner, Dr. J. W. Donnell of Clarkfield, who died by his own hand on June 11, 1898. Dr. Donnell was from Maine and came to Clarkfield around 1895 to help operate the B.H. Lewis Drug Store. He occupied rooms above this establishment and was a single man of forty-seven years of age. He was elected coroner of Yellow Medicine County in 1896, and one of the first cases he investigated was at the farm of Sivert Berg where four charred bodies were discovered in a barn fire. He was also coroner at the inquest of Louise Ott, who was brutally murdered by her husband in May 1898.

It was about 6 p.m. on Friday, June 11 when Dr. Kerkhoff went to check on Dr. Donnell, who was confined to his room with a terrible illness. The doctor found him lying on a cot, weltering in his own blood, which was flowing from a cut on the right side of his throat. He immediately called B.H. Lewis for assistance, and several other citizens arrived at the scene. While the wound was being sewed up, Donnell said he wished he had finished the job better, and it was no use to try to save him, as he had also taken a large dose of morphine. He said goodbye to the bystanders and asked them to notify his parents and brother in Maine. He then became unconscious and died within a few minutes. An examination showed that the jugular vein had been severed; the instrument used was a pair of pocket scissors with one point broken off. County Attorney Volstead was immediately contacted but said an inquest was not necessary, as it was clearly a case of suicide.

His parents and brother were notified, and they wired instructions to have the remains sent to Richmond, Maine. An undertaker was brought out from Montevideo, who embalmed the body, and it was sent east on the morning train.

For the past few weeks, Dr. Donnell had complained a great deal about not feeling well and had been drinking heavily. His business was in a slump, and he was very despondent. He had been heard to remark that if he could not make a living in Clarkfield, he would never try another place.

POKER GAME GONE BAD

POKER WAS FIRST played in New Orleans in the early 1800s. The actual name "poker" came from the French word "poque" or "pochen." Prior to the Civil War, poker spread quickly from New Orleans to towns throughout the Western frontier. The West was comprised largely of speculators and travelers, and both groups enjoyed gambling. In the early days, cheating was rampant, as were the murders of the cheaters, if they were caught. Gambling was viewed to be comprised of two distinct groups. There was the "player," who was a gentleman who enjoyed this type of entertainment, and there was the professional gambler whose aim was to make money without any regard to moderation or propriety. Professional gamblers contributed nothing to society. The public viewed their practice as nothing more than one man trying to con another out of his hard-earned money. Professional gamblers were known to cheat to win money from their victims. Western towns passed ordinances against gambling, and many towns kicked out known gamblers. Some gamblers were tarred and feathered, and it was common for vigilante groups to lynch them. The early frontier was a gambler's circuit. Wyatt Earp and Wild Bill Hickok were the first known professional poker players. Poker Alice was the first known female professional poker player. Hickok was shot in the back and died in a poker game in 1876 holding what was known as the "Dead Man's Hand" aces and eights.

Dr. Sigmund Wintner was born in Kentucky in 1867, the oldest of five children (Sigmund, Helene, Hugo, Louis, and Florence) born to Jewish parents, Leopold and Betty Wintner, who immigrated from Hungary in 1863. Leopold Wintner received his degree as a Doctor of Philosophy, and as a rabbi, his family moved throughout the South and Midwest, first to Mobile, Alabama in 1867, then Louisville, Kentucky in 1868, then Jackson, Mississippi in 1870, St. Paul, Minnesota in 1871, and Detroit, Michigan in 1873.

When the Wintners lived in Detroit Michigan, they employed a German woman by the name of Mary Sink as their maid. She seemed to be very pleasant and enjoyed serving the Wintners' every need. In 1874, Mary had relations with a young man who addressed her with offers of marriage, but whom, for some unexplained reason, she did not regard favorably. About 1:05 a.m. on August 13, 1874, Officer John Hogan saw a woman running through West Grand Circus Park in Detroit. She had very little clothing on, and Hogan, suspecting she meant mischief, ran after her at full speed. Before Hogan could reach her, she had thrown off all her clothing and plunged, with a loud shriek, headlong into the basin of the fountain where the water was only two feet deep. It appeared to be an attempted suicide. The officer leaped into the water, lifted her up, and shouted for help. Drs. Gilbert and Bailey arrived at the scene and revived the woman sufficiently for her to state her name and where she lived. A policeman was sent to the Wintner residence where he learned that the woman was a servant for the family. Leopold Wintner came at once with the policeman and took Mary Sink to the St. Mary's Hospital, where she lived only a few minutes. After her death, her remains were taken to the morgue. At 9 a.m. Coroner Griffin held an inquest and the jury rendered a verdict that Mary Sink came to her death while "temporarily insane." She was twenty-seven years old, had been in the United States only one year, and lived with the Wintner family. Just how this mental breakdown occurred was not known, but it was certain that for two or three days immediately preceding her death, she had manifested marked symptoms of insanity.

In 1876, the family made the decision to sell all their possessions and move back to Hungary. The youngest child, Florence, was born there in 1877. Leopold and his eldest son, Sigmund, who was eleven years old at the time, returned to New York on September 11, 1878. They left behind Betty, who was seven months pregnant at the time, along with the three younger children. Leopold left the family behind to accept a position as rabbi at Temple Beth Elohim in Brooklyn, New York and the rest of the family would make the journey later. It was in September 1879, when Betty and the four children, with Florence only ten months old, returned to New York to join Leopold and Sigmund. Leopold remained rabbi in Brooklyn for over twenty years. The Wintners were one of the prominent families in New York at that time. Sigmund's sister, Helene, became a well-known actress in theater in Brooklyn and Sigmund's brother, Hugo, also started out on the stage, but eventually became a lawyer, then assistant district attorney, and later a supreme court judge. Leopold at first strongly opposed Helene's career, but finding her determined, eventually consented. Helene was very talented and took the leading role in many performances. She became a member of the prestigious Amaranth and Toll Gate Inn companies.

Betty Wintner died in 1884 when Sigmund was only seventeen years old. This was devastating for him as he had a very close relationship with his mother.

In 1889, Sigmund graduated from New York College of Dentistry as a Doctor of Dental Surgery, practicing dentistry in Brooklyn for a few years. Later he moved to St. Paul for a brief time and then transferred his business to Minneapolis, forming a partnership with Dr. Douglas for about three years. Dr. Wintner was returning home from Minneapolis on a November evening in 1896 when he struck up a conversation with a man seated behind him on the trolley. They had supper together, talked for quite some time, and several hours later, Wintner left. As the doctor walked down the street, Lieutenant Pothen and another police officer from St. Paul came up behind him, struck him in the head behind the ear, and arrested him. Wintner was dumbfounded and wanted to know why he was being arrested. The officers told him he was arrested for being a "confidence man." At that time, a "confidence man" was a swindler who exploits the confidence of his victim, or a "con man." They took him to the police station, searched him, and put him upstairs in a cell. At 4 a.m., a friend of Wintner's got him released on $10 bail, which was to cover the charge they had against him. But when the case came up in municipal court a few days later, Wintner found out he was charged with being drunk. Somehow, Wintner proved that he had not been drinking that night. The case was about to be postponed for three days when Lieutenant Pothen wrote a letter to the judge explaining that it was all a horrible mistake. The judge immediately dismissed the case, and Wintner's mistaken arrest had finally ended.

Sometime in 1898, Wintner decided he needed a fresh start, leaving memories of his past behind. He spent time traveling the area in southwestern Minnesota, finally settling for the picturesque, friendly town of Granite Falls, located along the Minnesota River. Here was the place where he set up his dental practice. The first fifteen days of each month were spent at his office in Granite Falls and the remainder of the time spent at small towns in the area. He also set up a second office in Renville, a nearby town, spending ten days each month at that location.

It was known for years that the town of Granite Falls had been infested with a certain class of men who had done much gambling but usually in rather a small way. Lately, many ugly rumors were floating about late night poker games and the large losses sustained by the unwary.

Dr. Wintner had a quick temper and somewhat erratic behavior at times. He seemed to live a life of gaming and gambling. He participated in chess and billiard tournaments and spent lots of time and money betting on horses at the race track. Wintner enjoyed his whiskey, along with playing his favorite game of cards—poker. Wintner was known to have poker games that lasted into the wee hours of the morning. On a cold, dark night in an office building in Granite Falls, five men were at a poker game that went horribly wrong. It seemed that two of the men were said to be card sharks, unbeknownst to Dr. Wintner and the others in the game that night.

There are two versions explaining the presence of the professional card sharks in Granite Falls on that fateful night. Newspaper reports indicate that Dr. Wintner, Patrick Greer, Charles Galvin, Matt McCarthy, and others were accustomed to having poker games at which the stakes were sometimes high. News of these games got around, and a couple of professional gamblers from the Twin Cities heard of them and made their way to Granite Falls. These men were William Leonard (or Lenard), and William Stevenson, a professional ball player, who also went by the name William Mullane.

Another version of the gamblers' presence was that Wintner was often haughty and overbearing when he was winning, and that did not sit well with some of his fellow gamblers, who arranged for the professional gambler, Leonard, to come to Granite Falls to teach Wintner a lesson.

Whatever explanation for the gamblers' presence, William Leonard and William Stevenson arrived and checked into the Commercial Hotel where Wintner lived. Leonard was in the area for several weeks under the guise that he was a life insurance agent, and he was also in the employ of a secret service company. Leonard was said to have been smooth with cards and made considerable money at poker. The report had it that his success was due to dishonest methods of dealing. On Sunday, April 14, 1901, several men discussed getting together for a game of poker in the Commercial Hotel. But because Matt McCarthy had recently sold the hotel to his partner, he suggested the men find another place to play the game. Wintner offered his office as the perfect place to play poker, and the men agreed to meet there later that afternoon. The game began Sunday afternoon and continued until about 2:30 a.m. Monday morning, the 15th. By this time, Wintner had lost about $200, most of it to Leonard. Others in the game were William Stevenson, Charles Galvin, and Matt McCarthy. Patrick Greer, known as "The White Kid," watched the game but did not play or drink alcohol.

On several occasions during the game, Wintner commented that it was strange that every time he held kings, Leonard held aces, and this happened when Leonard dealt. At some point, Wintner left the table and went into an adjoining room. About ten minutes later, Wintner returned with a revolver, stuck it under Leonard's nose, and demanded $200. Wintner said, "The party has been robbed, and I want the boys' money back!" Leonard rose from his chair and leaped through the glass upper part of the door as Wintner called him to stop. Two shots were fired, hitting Leonard, who rolled to the bottom of the stairs, breaking his leg. Wintner reloaded the gun and pointed it at Stevenson. He again demanded his money and was handed $40, but later that night, Wintner returned the money to Stevenson.

McCarthy and Galvin ran down the stairs to see about Leonard, who lay at the bottom. He was conscious but bleeding profusely. Leonard handed Galvin a roll of bills, totaling $344, and told him to get the best doctor available, saying, "I guess I'm all through." Together with Stevenson, they carried him upstairs, where he was examined by Dr. Stratton before being taken to the Scheldrup Hospital. Leonard was found to have one bullet through the fleshy part of the right thigh, which had broken the bone, and another in the abdomen. Dr. Scheldrup, assisted by Dr. Rogers of Montevideo and Dr. Dunn of

Minneapolis, made as thorough an examination of Leonard as possible and felt he would not survive his injuries. Nine punctures were found in the intestines, and the bullet then passed through the liver and could not be located. Leonard died on Tuesday morning, April 16, around 9:30 a.m.

William Leonard was twenty-eight years old and called Denison, Iowa his home. His remains were brought to Denison for burial and the services were under the auspices of the Fraternal Order of Eagles of which he was a member in good standing. The services were conducted by Arthur M. White, who read the beautiful ritual of the order. Rev. A. G. Martyn was the officiating clergyman. There was something inspiring in the sight of those men paying their last respects to their dead brother, who would otherwise have been buried almost entirely among strangers. Mr. Leonard was agent for the Estherville Hail Insurance Company and was also in the employ of a secret service company. William Leonard, alias William Johnson, the "Irish Lord," was well educated, always elegantly dressed, wearing a Prince Albert coat with high hat, presenting a striking appearance.

After the shooting, Wintner went down stairs and up the street to meet Marshal Frank Dillingham, who was coming back from meeting the 2:30 a.m. Milwaukee passenger train. The marshal was informed that a man had been injured and was lying in the stairway. Dr. Wintner was arrested by Sheriff G.O. Homme in Michel's Saloon at 5:00 on the morning of the shooting and placed in jail. Judge Gorham Powers refused Wintner bail and excused himself from sitting on the case because of his acquaintance with the defendant.

The preliminary examination of the defendant came before J.L. Putnam, Justice of the Peace at 3 p.m. on April 15, 1901, held in the county jail building in Granite Falls. A.J. Volstead appeared as attorney for the State, and L.H. Schellbach appeared as attorney for the defendant. P.H. Greer, Matt McCarthy, William Stevenson, and C. Galvin were each duly sworn in at one time. After hearing witness testimonies and evidence presented at the proceedings, Wintner was charged with "assault in the first degree" and was bound over to the grand jury. When the grand jury heard the case in June, they brought in an indictment against Dr. Wintner of "murder in the first degree," due to the victim's demise. Wintner was held in the common jail in Granite Falls until his trial later that month.

The trial began on June 25, 1901, on the sultriest and most uncomfortable day of the year. The thermometer hovered around the century mark early in the morning. A strong breeze blew through the high windows of the courtroom, but it was like a blast from an oven. All day long lawyers, spectators, judge, and jury sweltered and perspired in the fierce heat and the ice water pitchers were emptied as fast as they were filled.

Promptly at 10 a.m. Judge Elliot of Minneapolis seated himself on the bench and the court was called to order. The judge was a tall, handsome-looking man, apparently not more than thirty-five years of age. The sheriff brought in the prisoner and seated him with his attorneys. Although the doctor's pallor and thin face showed that confinement was telling on him, his bearing was manly, and he smiled and bowed to friends and acquaintances around the room. As he entered, his father and sister were escorted by the bailiff to seats within the rail near the defendant.

County Attorney A.J. Volstead represented the State and was assisted by C.A. Foenes of Montevideo. Senator Schellbach of Granite Falls had nominal charge of the defense. The whole work of the defense fell on Frank Nye of Minneapolis, as the senator suffered from ill health and was able to stay in the courtroom only a brief time. Ole Hartwick of Granite Falls and Lieutenant Governor Smith of Montevideo also assisted him in the defense, making the most formidable array of legal talent that had been seen on one case in quite some time.

In his opening remarks, Attorney Volstead stated that "the State would prove murder and show that there was no provocation, such as the law will recognize, to justify the homicide. There was no sudden stress of passion, no sudden provocation, that the deed was done calmly and deliberately and that the consequences should be those of a deliberate act."

The state's first witness was Charles Galvin, a well-known saloon keeper in Granite Falls. Galvin stated that he entered the game about 10 p.m. It was around 2 a.m. when Wintner discovered that the cards were marked with a little punch on one edge. Wintner quit the game when he found the marked cards but sat and watched the others a few moments. It was crowded around the table, so Galvin asked Wintner to give him his place. Wintner got up then and went into another room. A few minutes later Wintner returned with a gun in his hand, which he pointed at Leonard and demanded the money he had lost. "You have robbed me of $200. I want you to return this money, and I will divide it among the patrons to whom it belongs." As soon as Leonard saw the gun, he quickly scooped up the money from the table and stuffed it into his pocket. Then he jumped at Wintner, pushing his chair back as he did so, and made a dash for the door, which was locked. Leonard threw up both hands and broke the glass, hanging in the door for just an instant. Wintner shot twice just at that moment. After the shots were fired, Wintner immediately turned the revolver upon Stevenson, saying, "Dig up!" and Stevenson dug up $40.

The next witness called was Patrick H. Greer (aka "Colonel"). He was the man who watched the game but did not play, because Leonard and Stevenson had cleaned him out the night before. His story of the occurrence was much the same as Galvin's. At this point, Bailiff Dillingham brought in a blue steel, Smith & Wesson revolver, double-action, .32-caliber, with a six-inch barrel. Greer was asked if he recognized the weapon, and said it was the gun used in the shooting. The weapon was marked "Exhibit B" and placed on the reporter's table. Greer stated that when he saw the gun, he shouted out, "My God, don't shoot, Doctor! I tried my best to get between them, but it was all too quick. I saw Leonard make a quick dart for the door and shouted again for the doctor not to fire, but the crash of the breaking glass and the two shots came as I spoke. Then I ran down the stairway to see about Leonard. I found him at the left of the entrance, half-lying on the sidewalk and groaning with pain. I asked Leonard if he was hurt, and he replied, 'I'm done for.' Then I rushed upstairs and told the players that Leonard was in bad shape. Then a couple of us carried him upstairs and I went for Dr. Stratton." On cross-examination, Mr. Nye brought out that all was friendly up to the moment of discovering the marked cards. Greer stated that he saw and handled the cards, and knew they were marked. Greer noted that all the men present drank liquor and there were several small, empty bottles scattered around the room.

The third witness called was Matt McCarthy, the former proprietor of the Commercial House. He was very calm and collected and weighed every question carefully before answering. His direct testimony brought out very little that was new except that Wintner, after he had fired the shots and held up Stevenson, walked into the laboratory and reloaded the revolver, saying as he did so, "We must have that fellow arrested—don't let him get away." McCarthy said he had just sold out his interest in the hotel to his partner and did not care to play there anymore. It was for this reason that he suggested they play at Wintner's office. It was the first time they had played there. McCarthy stated that he thought Wintner said, "Don't draw a gun," but was not positive. They were playing 50-cent jackpots. Wintner sat at Leonard's left hand, and when Leonard was dealing, Wintner would get two or more kings for openers, and invariably better his hand on the draw, but Leonard would always catch aces and rake in the pot. Wintner remarked about this and said to Leonard, "How is it you hold over me every time?" It was so unusual that everyone there remarked about it as well. McCarthy knew the cards were marked but was not positive who marked them.

William Stevenson (aka Mullane) was the next witness called by the state. He was also referred to as "Mullane" at the time of the occurrence. He was a tall, lanky youth, with a face marked with strong lines of dissipation. He was bright and quick, and his answers showed great shrewdness. Twice he refused to answer questions as to a conspiracy with Leonard to "do up the doctor," claiming it would incriminate himself, but the effect on the jury was the same as if he had answered the questions. His story of the shooting was the same as that of preceding witnesses up to the time of the shooting. Then he said that Wintner turned on him, saying, "Mullane, you dig up. You're just as much in this as Leonard is; now you give me that money."

"What did you do?" asked Mr. Volstead.

"I dug," was the prompt answer. "I was just putting on my hat when the doctor came out of the room with the revolver. The game had broken up because there was no heart in it after the doctor had discovered the marked cards. When the doctor came out with the gun, I laughed, and we all laughed, in fact, for we thought it was a joke. Wintner said, 'This is no joke, I want that money and I am in earnest.'"On cross-examination, Nye went after Stevenson's knowledge of marked cards. He stated that he knew the cards were marked; they were notched on the edge with a fingernail. The game was played on a small table with an under shelf on which the old packs had been thrown. Wintner went through the old packs and picked out the aces and kings by the notches on the back, saying as he did so, "Ain't they cute?" Leonard held aces over the doctor's kings every time he dealt, winning over $100 on one hand alone. When Wintner found out the cards were marked, he turned to Stevenson and said, "This is a nice proposition you have run in on us." He left the game immediately. Stevenson did not know whether Leonard was armed or not.

Stevenson stated he first got acquainted with Leonard on the train coming from St. Paul. They occupied the same car, and Leonard proposed they join forces to operate a little "smear" game, which required two players to be complete. As soon as Leonard dealt the cards, Stevenson knew him to be a cheater. The witness stated that he had intended to go over to Dakota, merely stopping at Granite Falls a night or two. There was always a good poker game in town, and he would rather play cards than eat.

"Dr. Wintner made the good poker game, didn't he?" asked Nye with a pleasant smile.

"There was always plenty of poker money here," said Stevenson.

Efforts by the defense attorney to introduce marked cards and the "mirror ring" worn by Leonard were ruled out. Defense attorney Schellbach was talented and experienced in the field of law. He introduced depositions taken of several witnesses for the defense as follows:

J.B. Richard, Captain of Police in Sioux City, Iowa, testified that William Leonard, alias, W.W. Barrett, was a scoundrel and in the business of being a "crook gambler and grafter." A grafter was one who gambles not on the square but induces others to enter games which have been prepared for trapping and defrauding the party induced. Richard first became acquainted with Leonard when he (Leonard) was arrested in Sioux City in 1898 on the charge of vagrancy. Leonard was found guilty and sentenced to ten days in the county jail and ordered by the police court, Judge Gray, to immediately leave the city when released from jail. Leonard had also been suspected of fleecing a party from Danbury out of $400, and a watch was put out on him by the local authorities there. Overall, Richard described Leonard as having a bad reputation, and that the gambling houses in Sioux City would not allow him to play in their rooms because of his well-known crookedness.

J.W. Bagley, ex-saloon keeper from St. Paul, stated that he knew William Stevenson and William Leonard as professional card players and gamblers. In that area, Leonard was also known as "Society Red," or the "Irish Lord." Bagley said Leonard was well-known as an expert manipulator of cards. Stevenson wanted Bagley to take a trip with him; he said we could do a good stroke of business in Minnesota and particularly in Granite Falls. Bagley stated, "I told him I could not go as my children were sick with scarlet fever. Stevenson said he was sure if

I were with him there would be no chance of losing, as he had located some good victims for poker that had plenty of money and we could do a good stroke of business as he had been over the field before and was well acquainted with all the poker fiends. Stevenson wanted me to help him skin these victims by crooked card manipulating at poker and other gambling games with cards."

Mrs. F.L. Horton, a dressmaker, stated that Leonard occupied rooms in her house for four years in Sioux Falls, South Dakota. She knew very little about his gambling habits but said that Leonard was known to carry enormous amounts of cash, from $500 to $1,500 on his person, and always carried a revolver when he went out. The day he left for Granite Falls, he had nearly $500, and a diamond stud that he wore on his shirt and carried a revolver. "Leonard always called me 'sister,' and 'mama,' and treated me as such," she said. Mrs. Horton was asked what she knew about Matt McCarthy and another person having taken some of the money belonging to Mr. Leonard after he was shot. She said, "I know very little, except Matt McCarthy was very anxious that I should get out of Granite Falls and he followed me and my daughter to Sioux Falls. I do not know if McCarthy took any of the money, but I was suspicious of him, because somebody took over $1,000, his diamond stud, and a revolver. At the time of Leonard's death, there was turned over to me $343 in receipts and money, there was $30 turned over to me in cash, and the rest was in receipts for money paid out, his two gold rings, a solid gold watch, and what clothing he had, and about $2,000 of paper that Mr. Leonard was supposed to have had for collection."

"What do you know about Leonard professing to be a detective?"

"Well, he was, he had a certificate, but I find on looking at his certificate, he had let it lapse, but he still wore his star when it was necessary," Mrs. Horton replied.

Pearl Strong, age seventeen, was Mrs. Horton's daughter. She stated that she knew very little about Leonard's gambling and playing cards, but stated he always carried a revolver and large sums of cash when he went out. Pearl said that the evening before Leonard left, they were sitting by the window and he was counting his money and there was $410 in the roll and some other change in his pocket. Pearl stated she and Leonard were engaged to be married on May 1, 1901. The only items Pearl received after Leonard's death was about $300 in notes and receipts.

"Did you receive a letter from Mr. Leonard asking you to send some instrument sharp at both ends and made of a metal for a clock spring?"

"Yes, I did."

"Do you have the instrument in your possession?" asked the attorney.

"No, sir, I have not."

"Have you the pattern from which it was made?"

"I have the pattern from which it was made and attach the same to this answer. It was made of aluminum, about 2 1/2 inches long and about 1/2 inch in width, forked at both ends, and each angle point very sharp. The points of each being over 1/2 inch in length."

The attorney asked the witness if she knew about Leonard's professing to be a detective. She stated that Leonard had been a detective since she'd known him. She said that he used to be on a ranch with Buffalo Bill and from there he went to be a detective.

The case was very hard-fought, and a brilliant array of legal counsel battled over the innocence or guilt of the prisoner. The defense attorneys set up a claim of justifiable homicide, that a plot had been formed in St. Paul by which Leonard was to come out to Granite Falls and by marked cards and other devices, fleece Wintner, and divide the spoils with Stevenson and McCarthy. Swindling at cards was a felony under the Minnesota statues, and so they argued that when Wintner found out he was being swindled, he had the same right to recover his

CRIME and CALAMITY

property or to prevent the swindler escaping with the property as if the felony had been committed in any other way--that the shooting to prevent the escape of Leonard after Leonard had refused to return the stolen money, was within his legal rights.

The prosecuting attorney, Mr. Volstead, found the theory of the defense a hard one to overthrow. There was no controversy over the evidence, and he was forced to fight the case before the jury on technical points as to the amount of violence necessary to prevent Leonard's escape and as to whether the felony committed by Leonard was complete before he left the room. Volstead was very savage in his handling of Wintner and placed him in as unfavorable a light as possible.

Nye made a very convincing plea for his client, and contrary to expectation, did not plea for sympathy, but forcibly argued the rights of the prisoner to defend his property rights as he did.

After closing arguments and just before supper, the judge charged the jury. His charge was fair and impartial and in no way calculated to guide the decision. The lightest sentence that might be imposed upon the defendant would be manslaughter.

About 11 p.m. that night, the court was again called to order, the prisoner was brought in, the jury filed into the box and the decision was announced -- "not guilty." Dr. Wintner was a free man. The verdict, which was thought by many to have been clearly contrary to the evidence, was a surprise even to Dr. Wintner's attorney, Frank Nye, who it was said, had hoped to accomplish little more than the saving of the doctor from too severe a sentence. The reason for the verdict was found to be in Nye's eloquence and expertise in presenting the case for the defense. Nye was said to have had the jury in tears a good deal of the time during his closing argument, and to have worked upon their feelings so that they were blind to the cold, hard facts of the evidence presented, and therefore, set Dr. Wintner free. The verdict returned by the jury was unexpected and most decidedly unpopular. The excitement in the community around Granite Falls and Renville had heated up considerably; threats of lynching Wintner were heard, and even the jurymen were reported to have fled into the woods, fearing harsh treatment at the hands of indignant citizens.

After Wintner was set free, Attorney Volstead admitted that he kept his finger on the public pulse and knew of the bitter feeling against Wintner. Volstead, in view of the sentiment of the community, immediately issued a warrant, charging Wintner with "robbery in the first degree" against Stevenson during the poker game that night. But after Volstead consulted with the sheriff, and in view of the possible difficulty of convicting Wintner on such a charge, decided not to pursue Wintner or make any further effort to serve the warrant.

In every respect, this was a queer case, but the jury based its verdict, claiming in a "gentlemanly game of poker" it was too much to expect that in the normal run of affairs, one poker player should receive two kings for seven consecutive deals, while another gambler, in the same game, received two aces.

The outcome of this trial was the subject of spirited conversation for many days, and some of the sentiment toward the doctor was not friendly. Wintner's friends feared for his safety, so in the darkness of a June night, a group of men got a team of horses and buggy together and took Wintner to Clarkfield, where he caught the night train to New York. Sigmund moved in with his father in Brooklyn. In August 1901, Wintner was arrested in Brooklyn on the charge of larceny. Nothing more about this arrest appeared in the newspapers. Maybe the case was dismissed due to Wintner's family prominence; no one is quite sure. Sigmund never again visited Granite Falls, and the farm he once owned was finally sold to other parties in June 1902. Wintner continued his gambling habits, never married, and lived in boarding houses. The 1930 and 1940 census had him living in Miami Beach, Florida. At some point, Wintner returned to Manhattan, New York where he passed away at the age of eighty-four.

This certainly was a bad case any way you look at it, and it was unfortunate that it happened, but though the verdict may not have been just, and that human life may have been held lightly in this case, no one would look at Dr. Wintner and say he would not suffer for the remainder of his existence. It appears the family's prestige and wealth relieved him of sustaining punishment for any of his crimes. However, he could never wash his hands of the blood of the human life he took on that fateful night in a poker game gone bad.

Sketch of Dr. Sigmund Wintner
(from St. Paul Globe, April 17, 1901)

RAIDED THE BLIND PIG

THE "BLIND PIG," also called "blind tiger" or "speakeasy," was an illicit establishment that sold alcoholic beverages during the Prohibition era (1920-1933). The term "blind pig" originated in the United States in the 19th century. It was applied to lower-class establishments, and the operator of a saloon or bar would charge customers to see an attraction (such as an animal and most times a pig) and then serve a complimentary alcoholic beverage, thus circumventing the law. The alcohol itself could be called "booze" or "giggle-juice," but "hooch," named for alcohol made by the Hoochinoo Indians in Alaska, was a more accurate word for the low-quality, homemade variety. People who sold liquor were called "bootleggers" because boots were a favorite hiding place for booze.

Andrew Volstead, Granite Falls resident, was most noted for introducing the National Prohibition Act, also known as the Volstead Act, to enforce the Eighteenth Amendment, which prohibited the production, sale, and transport of intoxicating liquors. The act was ratified and went into effect in 1920. The Volstead Act was later repealed, ending Prohibition in 1933.

The following story appeared in the *Reform Advocate*, Clarkfield newspaper, dated September 26, 1901. It was a very significant article for its time because it occurred in the early days before the height of the Prohibition era, and it gives a glimpse into what the "blind pig" was all about.

For many weeks in late summer 1901, the number of drunken men on the streets of Clarkfield had been steadily increasing. At all hours of the night, the sounds of carousing could be heard along the dark alleys, and the reputation of the town was fast becoming a stench in every man's nostrils.

The "blind pig" in the building known as the "Clarkfield Glass Block" was raided on Saturday evening September 21, 1901, for securing evidence proving that it was a place where intoxicating liquors were unlawfully sold. The raid had been planned for earlier in the week, but the councilmen thought it would be better to wait until Saturday night as they would be more liable to find a supply of "wet goods" on hand. The raid was a success and while the events which followed were not altogether satisfactory, the town of Clarkfield had the satisfaction of knowing that the owners of the establishment had been arrested and fined and that the "pig" had been closed.

In 1899, the legislature passed a law which gave justices of the peace the right to issue search warrants by which "blind pigs" could be searched for liquor, and the liquor, along with the fixtures in the place, could be sold or destroyed. The law had its good points, but the way in which it was drawn up was hardly commendable. It would puzzle anyone but a thoroughly educated attorney to draw up a complaint by it. Anticipating this raid, Justice Shaw had contacted the county attorney for advice and the proper forms of complaint and warrant, but these had not been received before the raid. On the night of the raid, the councilmen called on Justice Shaw and asked to have papers made out under the new law, and Shaw did his best to make them out. They were placed in the hands of Constable Quesnell for service. The councilmen and Shaw went along to be of assistance during the raid.

That Saturday night, the business was good at the Glass Block. A crowd of men stood four deep in front of the bar and three men in their shirtsleeves were working hard, opening bottles and filling glasses. A fair percent of the crowd showed the effects of something stronger than hop tea. R.G. Falk, one of the proprietors, was outside when the officers arrived but left quite suddenly. S.J. Severson, the other proprietor, was in the room, and Constable Quesnell read him the warrants. Severson invited the officers to look around as much as they chose. They could find only empty bottles. Piles of these stood in every corner and in long rows behind the bar. Thirty barrels filled with them stood outside in the backyard. But of full bottles, there was not so much as a shadow. Still, in some mysterious way, the bottles kept coming up behind the bar and the corks kept popping. Somebody invited Mr. Orwoll to take a drink and he took it—bottle and all, keeping it for evidence. The rest of the party was inquiring of Severson what was in the next building. He said there was nothing but some stored furniture and carriage paints. But the constable was not satisfied and insisted on going in. Severson said that the place was locked, and that Falk had the keys. There was nothing left to do but break in the door. Constable Quesnell picked up an ax from the woodpile nearby and struck a few good blows on the lock. The door flew in with a bang, and the officers entered. It was pitch dark, but after a few moments searching for the switch, the lights were turned on. Three of the four rooms within the building were a scene of confusion. Sawdust and empty barrels and bottles lay everywhere. Someone whispered something about a "small room." Mr. Orwoll located this and crawled in through a sliding door about three feet high. The others heard him say, "We've looked far enough." In the center of the floor stood a tub of water in which two dozen bottles were cooling, and the label on them read "Golden Grain

Belt Beer." Three barrels filled with bottled beer stood along the wall—evidence enough to "pull" a dozen places.

Severson and four others were immediately placed under arrest, but one, Julius Corson, escaped on the pretense of going for his coat and had not been seen since. Constable Quesnell sent for the dray, and the stuff was taken to the jail. Although it was very late, the prisoners were brought into the justice's office and tried. Severson plead guilty to a charge, brought under the village ordinance, of selling intoxicating liquor without a license. Oscar Kjos and Gust Olson were held for trial until the following week. Severson paid his fine, $25, and costs and was discharged. R.G. Falk was arrested on Sunday morning, September 22, as he was leaving his residence for Montevideo. He gave bonds to appear the following morning. County Attorney Volstead was telephoned and promised to be present. On September 23rd, Falk appeared with Attorney Haugland of Montevideo. Volstead told the council that he didn't believe it advisable to bring an action under the state law, so a new complaint was made out, charging Falk with a violation of the village ordinance, prohibiting the sale of intoxicating liquor. Falk pled guilty to this charge and was fined $25 and costs.

This was the first of the "blind pig" raids. The Clarkfield councilmen would say that it would be dangerous for anyone to try to run a place for the unlawful sale of intoxicating liquor in this town hereafter. Every place of suspicious appearance would be closely watched, and if it appeared that any liquor was being sold there, it would be promptly raided. And the next time the proper papers would be prepared by the county attorney and would be guaranteed to stick.

THE JAIL IS BURGLARIZED

ON THE SAME night as the raid, several thirsty fellows broke into the Clarkfield Jail and took about a dozen bottles of beer from one of the barrels of the stash that was confiscated in the raid at the Glass Block earlier that evening. From the number of empty bottles found around the jail, it was quite evident that the beer was taken to be drunk only on the premises. Immediately, a new and much stronger lock was put on the door, and the following night, the marshal was put in charge of the building and its contents. Either through a misunderstanding of his instructions or for reasons best known to himself, he did not watch the jail very closely, because somebody broke the new lock, and this time all the rest of the beer was taken, except for six bottles. Of course, it was a good joke on the village officers but liable to prove an expensive joke to the perpetrators. The council was not willing to let the matter rest and felt the crime a serious one, amounting to burglary. As far as could be determined, the burglars were never apprehended, but you can bet they had themselves a rollicking good time drinking up the evidence confiscated from the blind pig raid.

Main Street in Clarkfield, c. 1900s
(photo from Yellow Medicine County Historical Society collection)

STRANGE DISAPPEARANCE

JOHN SWENSON WAS one of the first settlers in Norman Township in 1872. He secured a homestead on section 4, where the City of Canby now stands. He erected a shanty and for the convenience of his neighbors, opened a little store in his cabin. In November of 1874, he secured the establishment of a post office at his store, which at his suggestion was named Canby, in honor of General E.R.S. Canby, whom Modoc Indians in Northern California had assassinated the year before. By 1876, the surrounding country was receiving new settlers, and the railway company deemed it time to begin the operation of train service over the western part of the line. Canby Station was established, and on August 24, 1876, the Winona & St. Peter Railroad Company platted the town site. Because of its location on the rail line, Canby grew quickly and was incorporated as a village in 1879 and as a city in 1905.

It was rumored that J.H. Gehbauer, city engineer of Canby, had disappeared, and there was a published statement to that effect in the

Canby newspapers. It was first thought that there might be foul play, but after all circumstances became known, it appeared to be a plain case of desertion of payment of contracted debts. Mr. Gehbauer was well-known, lived in Granite Falls, and served as county supervisor of highways. Gehbauer was from Austria; he came to this country in 1909 and located in Texas. He was twenty-seven years old, of an eccentric character, and small of stature, being about the size of a ten-year-old boy. He was conscious of his physical handicaps but remained self-assertive. His attitude was such that he was generally respected, manifested a degree of more than average intelligence, had a good command of the English language, and had the reputation of being proficient in his work as an engineer.

It was reported that Gehbauer left Canby on December 16, 1916, drove to Granite Falls, and left his car at Lende & Knudson's for repairs which totaled $75. From there, he telephoned M.N. Thompsen of Canby, and asked him to go to Taunton to make sure that his new $3,600 ditching machine, which had been shipped to that place, was properly stored for the winter. According to the Canby newspapers, Gehbauer owed $70 for office rent and various sums to other parties, totaling probably over $1,000. He had paid $500 down on the ditching machine, which was money he borrowed, and was to pay another $500 once the machine was delivered to him. From all reports, it seemed he was doing well, having much work to do. Thus, his sudden disappearance for the sake of avoiding payment of his bills came as quite a shock to the community. Gehbauer was never seen or heard from again. His disappearance remains a mystery.

Main Street in Canby, c. 1909
(photo from Yellow Medicine County Historical Society collection)

CRIME and CALAMITY

GAMBLING IN A BOX CAR

AT THE JUNCTION of the Minneapolis & St. Louis and the Great Northern Railways, on the southwest quarter of section 12, Sandnes Township, and on the south bank of the Yellow Medicine River, is the village of Hanley Falls. The Minneapolis & St. Louis Railroad was built in the summer of 1884. At the time of the selection of the townsite, the name of Halley Falls had not been thought of. The first name suggested was to call the station "Cable" in honor of the president of the railroad, but Cable raised objection to the use of his name. Then "Cleveland" was suggested, but another town in the state had already secured that name. Finally, the name "Hanley" was selected in honor of another railroad official. To make Hanley more distinctive, "Falls" was added to the name in 1886. One might believe that there was a waterfall on the Yellow Medicine River, but this was not the case; the river flowed peacefully on its course. Hanley Falls was platted by Charles F. Hatch on September 8, 1884.

An altercation arose in a railroad bunk car at Hanley Falls between Algot Johnson, Great Northern bridge foreman, and Theodore Holme, a Hanley Falls resident on December 20, 1916. The trouble arose, according to Johnson, by his demanding that Holme and a member of the crew cease matching money in the bunk car, as he did not allow gambling.

The story as told by Algot Johnson was that he had gone into Hanley Falls to see who he could pick up to help with work at the train yard. He met Theodore Holme on the street and asked him if he wanted some work. Holme said he wasn't sure, as it was rather cold for outside work, but he walked down with Johnson to the bunk cars on the track, and while Johnson went about other business, Holme went into the car. When Johnson came by later to check on things, he found Holme and a member of the crew matching money. He told them to quit, as he did not allow gambling in the cars. At this time, two men turned on him. He succeeded in throwing the bridge man out the door, but Holme grabbed a chair and used it as a weapon. He backed Johnson around in the car and finally into a corner by his bunk. Fearing for his life, Johnson said he reached into the bunk and grabbed a gun, demanding that Holme put down the chair and get out. Holme rushed at him and Johnson fired, the bullet striking the man in the abdomen and lodging in his back. Following the shooting, aid was summoned. Holme was taken to the Marshall Hospital, Lyon County, where surgery was performed to extract the bullet. It was determined that the wound was not fatal.

Johnson gave himself up to the Hanley Falls marshal. He was brought to Granite Falls that evening on the freight train and placed in jail. The hearing would not be held until the condition of the injured man was known. The case was brought to court on January 17, 1917. After all the evidence was presented, the jury returned a verdict of not guilty, and Algot Johnson walked out of jail a free man. According to the evidence, there had been some liquor consumed in the crew car that evening, and it appeared Johnson acted in self-defense when he pulled a gun and shot Holme through the abdomen. Sometime later, Johnson and Holme made amends, and all was forgiven. Holme continued to enjoy liquor at times but never participated in a game of cards ever again.

Minneapolis & St. Louis Railway Station
Hanley Falls Depot, c. 1900s
(photo from Yellow Medicine County Historical Society collection)

FROZE TO DEATH

DR. POLLOCK OF Hanley Falls was called out to aid a sick family living seven miles west and one mile south of Hanley Falls on February 3, 1917. The doctor hired Ryan, the livery driver, and in a cutter, they arrived at the house at 8 p.m. to attend to the sick person. Dr. Pollock visited with the family after administering some medicine to their very ill daughter, who had a high fever.

Dr. Pollock and Ryan left the house about 10:30 p.m. during a heavy snowstorm. After having gone some distance, the cutter tipped over from the steep grade and the two men decided to unhitch the horses and ride into town on horseback. Ryan led the way with the understanding that the doctor was to follow directly behind him. After traveling some distance, Ryan lost the doctor, and although he retraced his journey, could not find him. Ryan hit a snowdrift and was thrown off and couldn't find his horse. He stayed in that place thinking that the doctor would be somewhere around, but no one showed up, so Ryan started out and hit a fence through which he crawled and ended up at the river. He walked back and forth along the river all night; he didn't know where he was. Ryan was snow blind by morning but finally managed to find a house where he told them about the missing doctor. Ryan suffered from frostbite on his hands and feet.

A large search party was organized, but the blizzard was so bad there was not a chance of conducting any kind of thorough search. The following day, the search continued. The doctor was found about 11:40 that morning, three miles west and half a mile north of Cottonwood, Lyon County. He was frozen stiff. His horse was found dead in a snow bank about a quarter mile from him. Dr. Pollock was a young man of thirty-two and had lived in Hanley Falls only about four months, coming from a small town near New Ulm, Brown County.

TRAIN WRECK NEAR ECHO

THE VILLAGE OF Echo, named after the township in which it was situated, was founded in August 1884 when the Minneapolis & St. Louis (M&STL) Railway was built through the county. The M&STL conducted a survey of the western part of the state in 1883. The outcome of the survey determined that a rail line that would pass to the west via the Echo area could be accomplished. The proposed stations along the railway would be Echo, Wood Lake, Hanley Falls, Hazel Run, and Clarkfield. The founding of Echo was simultaneous with the arrival of the railroad. The townsite, owned by the railroad company, was platted September 8, 1884 and the sale of lots began. The railroad was most important to the development of the town, having been established by the railroad as a shipping point. Despite working through bankruptcy for many years, the M&STL continued to serve the villages, carrying passengers and hauling freight along the route. In the late 1930s, the news of abandonment of the line became a possibility. As highways in the state began to improve, distribution of freight via truck was more economical and efficient and was in direct competition with the train system. On July 20, 1960, the passenger train service ceased operation.

The freight trains continued to run into the 1970s until the Chicago & Northwestern Railroad bought out the Minneapolis & St. Louis Railway. The railway was in business from 1870 to 1960. Today, the railroad is still in service on a limited basis.

The following story is from the *Echo Enterprise*, date unknown.

Probably the most exciting event which happened near the tiny, quiet town of Echo occurred one Friday afternoon about 3:40 p.m. Due to a severe snowstorm, the cuts were all full of snow; the eastbound passenger train, being obliged to buck her own way through the drifts, was already about five hours behind schedule when it left Wood Lake. They had done considerable shoveling and had got along well until they struck the cut two and a half miles west of Granite Falls, when they discovered one side of the track was covered about six feet deep and the other rail was nearly bare. The train plowed into the drift at about forty miles an hour and might have succeeded in getting through despite the hard drift, had not one side of the snowdrift given way and fallen under the wheels. When the forward trucks of the engine struck the obstruction, she flew the track and tore out one or two lengths of rail. The front trucks of the tender jumped the rail, and the iron horse started across the prairie with her nose in the frozen ground. One of the cylinders burst, but there was no explosion. The engineer was violently thrown through the glass at the side of the cab and landed about twenty feet away upon the snow packed ground. He was not seriously hurt but suffered a few bruises. The fireman was thrown against the front end of the boiler but rebounded and fell with one arm between the engine and the oncoming tender, where he was pinned. The timbers had to be raised or cut away before he could be released, and this took nearly an hour, during which time he had to lie there exposed to the icy wind. Those who saw him thought he could never survive the ordeal, but when he was released, it was found that he had luckily found the only place where he could have been thus caught and not had his arm crushed. Had his arm been three inches either way, it would have severed the arteries, and he would have bled to death before he could have been reached. His nose was broken, and he was considerably cut about the face, but under the circumstances it was a miracle that he escaped with his life.

Minneapolis & St. Louis Railway Station
Echo depot, c. 1900s
(photo from Yellow Medicine County Historical Society collection)

CRIME and CALAMITY

JUSTIFIABLE HOMICIDE

I**T WAS REPORTED** in the *Granite Falls Tribune* on February 6, 1917, that a former resident, Frank Miller, had been shot by a Montana sheriff as a criminal. Miller left Granite Falls in 1913 after working two years for S.N. Holliston as a painter. He was a rather tall, slender man with dark hair and sandy mustache. After leaving Granite Falls, he moved to Hanley Falls and married a respectable girl but then left after living with her for a year or so. From Hanley Falls, he went to Echo, where he engaged in the painting business under the name of Watrous, and from Echo moved to Cottonwood and started a restaurant. He left Cottonwood in 1915 and had not been heard from since. It seems that Miller, as he was known here, went under any number of aliases. According to Malcolm Holliston, for whom Miller once worked, he explained his different names by saying his mother had been married five times and he could use any of the five names he wished.

The following was the article from the *Granite Falls Tribune*.

J.E. Watrous, wanted by Sheriff Jack Bennett of Sheridan County for horse stealing was fatally shot by Deputy Sheriff Jack

Teal. The man shot, though supposed mortally wounded, lived until last night, having been brought to the Deaconess Hospital for medical attention.

Sheriff Powell had information and a request to be on the lookout for Watrous for four or five days prior to the shooting. He also had a complete detailed description of him, and of a horse, saddle, bridle and 30-30 rifle stolen recently. After this information was received, along with a statement that Sheriff Bennett of Sheridan County held a warrant for his arrest, search was at once instituted. After ascertaining that the man had been in Glasgow, Montana, Deputy Teal and Jailor Dickman were detailed to run him down and arrest him. The trail of the man who was riding the stolen horse was followed east of town until a lone horseback rider was sighted about twelve miles southeast. The officers came up to him in the immediate vicinity of the Barton schoolhouse near the Russell farm. Teal called to the man that he wanted him, and for a reply, the crack of a rifle over the shoulder came, followed by a rifle shot from Teal. As the victim was about to fire again, another shot from Teal sent him reeling to the ground. He admitted his identity, complaining that he had not been shot higher up and further stated that he would rather be dead than alive. A rig was secured, and the wounded man brought to the hospital and given every medical attention possible, but he died a brief time later. Rev. R. H. Stone who visited him in the hospital stated he had a wife and child in Minnesota and that he had a mother but did not know where she was and a sister. At the coroner's inquest, the jury rendered a verdict of "justifiable homicide" the horse thief having met death while resisting an officer of the law.

COMMITTED AS INSANE

IN FEBRUARY 1918, Ralph Crosby was brought to Granite Falls from Hanley Falls to be examined as to his sanity. Crosby told Judge Hall that he was a murderer and told in detail of a horrible crime. The judge, as well as, the examining doctors and County Attorney Bengtson, took the man's story as the ravings of a crazy man and committed him to the St. Peter asylum. Sometime later, word was received that the man's story was true and that extradition papers had been processed so that he might be taken back to answer for the crime.

Crosby had been employed as renter on a farm belonging to O.G. Veldy in Hanley Falls. His remarks about detectives constantly following him finally led to his being brought to Granite Falls by Marshal Harris two weeks previously. Crosby was examined at that time but was discharged as sane. A week later Crosby was again brought to Granite Falls for the examination that led to his commitment.

According to the story told by Ralph Leonard Crosby (or Crane), he was born somewhere but did not know exactly where. His age was about twenty-six or twenty-eight years old, but he did not know which. He had been a soldier of fortune traveling over the entire country, had served four years in the regular army, had worked in Texas, Illinois, Iowa, Canada, International Falls, where he was married to Mildred Hillstrom, and then the couple moved to Hanley Falls where he secured work on a farm.

Ralph Leonard Crosby aka Roy L. Clark's confession was published in daily papers on the day it was made:

> *St. Peter, Minn., February 2, 1918 – Ralph L. Crosby committed to the state asylum here January 29, from Yellow Medicine County, confessed to authorities there today, the murder of John Bell and his wife in Red Oak, Iowa in August 1914. In response to a telegram from Sheriff R.A. Dunn of Montgomery County, Iowa, the officials here were holding Crosby. That while in Yellow Medicine County, Crosby feared detectives were after him, told his wife of the crime and through his actions was declared insane and brought here.*

This crime was committed by Roy L. Clark and took place on the evening of August 22, 1914. The farm on which the awful tragedy occurred comprised 200 acres and belonged to Edward and Gordon Hayes of Red Oak, Iowa. The farm was located about eight and a half miles northeast of Red Oak and three and a half miles north of Stanton in a secluded spot, cut off from nearly all outside communication. Mr. and Mrs. John T. Bell had recently moved to this place from Missouri. Clark was a new farmhand and managed the property. He had left a grading crew to take employment on the Bell place. He lived with the Bell family on the property and seemed to have no trouble with them in the slightest. But he got the idea in some unaccountable manner that they had it in for him, and his hallucination got the better of his judgment until he was finally prompted to attempt their extermination. At the supper table that night, he thought he detected the mother and girls exchanging glances which were of a significant nature and he secretly vowed to kill the whole family. After supper he sat and played on the mouth harp for a while, and then at about 8:30 p.m., all retired.

It was a hot night, John and Carrie Bell slept in the south room, and pulled their bed into the middle of the room to get some air. Their four-year-old daughter, Della, slept on a cot nearby. The two older girls, Vina and Nettie, went to bed in the west room and they, too, pulled their bed into the middle of the room. Clark, whose room was upstairs over the girls' room, went up to his room, took off his shoes and waited for the folks downstairs to get into bed. Then when all was still and dark, he took his automatic shotgun, loaded it, and with a flashlight to guide his steps, slipped downstairs in his stocking feet and while standing at the foot of the bed where the couple slept, shot John Bell three times and his wife, Carrie, twice. Some of the shot passed into the room occupied by the girls, penetrating the window shade on the west window and breaking the mirror in a dresser which sat in the southwest corner. The slayer gave the defenseless couple no opportunity to escape, and when he had finished his heinous work, their corpses lay in a pool of their own blood, frightfully mutilated. The murderer's first shot took effect in Mr. Bell's knee and the girls in the next room heard him cry out with pain. The second shot put him out of his agony, the charge taking effect in his left side, breaking several ribs and mangling his arm. A third shot penetrated his right side in a similar manner. Mrs. Bell was shot once in the armpit and once in the back, and it was thought she was either lying on her side or had made a move after the first shot. With his gun empty, Clark returned to his room and placed three more loads in the chamber, returning to kill the girls. As he stepped into their bedroom, he brazenly announced that he had come to kill them too, and the poor, helpless girls, trembling with fear, drew the covers up over their heads and awaited their doom, but the murderer did not shoot, he seemed to be weakening. And then it was Nettie, fifteen years of age, who became a heroine. With wonderful courage and a God-given presence of mind, she threw back the covers, got out of bed, and went toward the murderer. She did not go hastily, nor as one in fear, but she went with outstretched arms, and with love in her voice. She told him they were not ready to die, and she begged him to spare their lives. And to that innocent girl the fiendish murderer replied, "You girls have brought this on yourselves."

Nettie did not waver. "Why, Roy, what have we done to bring this on?" she asked.

"Oh, you know," he said. "You don't treat me right, and you don't like me, and so I decided to kill you." And with that, he thrust the barrel of his gun against her face with so much force that the bruise was still visible.

Nettie then threw her arms around Roy's neck and pleaded with him again. "Roy, it is not true, it is not true!" she said. "We like you and we have always liked you. Roy, you are losing your mind. Something is the matter with you. We never intended to harm you, and please spare our lives, Roy, please!"

At this time, Della, climbed down from her cot and called "Mama." The words went to the heart of the murderer like a bolt of lightning. He winced, and the two older girls kept up their pleading. The toddler went to her mother and threw her arms around her neck, but the only answer to her wailing cry was the feeling of warmth from her mother's life blood. The little tot came to the room where her two sisters were still begging for mercy and Vina, seventeen years old, with an even voice and a bravery as great as her sister's, called to the child to come in. If the worst happened, at least they would all go together.

"Honest, Roy, we like you," pleaded Nettie, "and we don't want to be killed."

Then Roy lowered his gun and hung his head. "Well," he said, "if that's the case, I'm sorry I killed your father and mother. Perhaps you had better call some of the neighbors and tell them about it." So, Roy went out into the yard, got down on one knee and set the muzzle of the gun against his temple, put the finger on the trigger, and just then thought the girls were in trouble now and would need help. At that moment, Roy decided not to kill himself. Instead he sat down on the grass with the gun in his lap.

The girls then went to the phone and called the neighbor, Edward Bailey, and told him to come over right away, but they did not say what the trouble was for fear Roy would return to finish the job. Mr. Bailey got up and immediately got dressed, and with his wife they started for the Bell home. They carried a lantern as they walked along the road. They wondered if Mr. Bell had been kicked by a horse or if Mrs. Bell had become suddenly ill. They hurried as fast as they could and in less than twenty minutes were at the Bell home, but during this time another drama was being enacted at the Bell home.

Vina and Nettie Bell were two of the bravest women this world has ever known. After calling the Baileys to rush over, the girls, following up the advantage they had gained, did not permit Roy to escape, nor did they try to flee for fear they would be shot. In the awful silence of that house of carnage, they tiptoed out of the house and onto the porch and clad only in their nightgowns, they took seats directly in front of the person who had brutally killed their parents less than five minutes before. There on the porch they sat and there on the grass the murderer sat less than fifteen feet away. In the dim starlight they could see every movement he made and knew he still held his gun. Five minutes passed, it seemed an age. Anxiously the girls looked down the road for some sign of approaching relief. They stoically sat and listened for some sound in the night to tell them help was on the way. Ten minutes passed, another age and still the murderer sat on the grass making no effort to leave nor any gesture of further violence. No light. No sound. Fifteen minutes passed and finally the girls discerned a light coming down the road and Mr. and Mrs. Bailey appeared.

Clark was the first to greet them. "Hello, Roy," they said. "What's the matter?"

"Oh, I just killed Mr. and Mrs. Bell, but I wish I had the last few minutes of my life to live over and I wouldn't have done it."

"No, you don't mean that, do you, Roy?" asked Mr. Bailey who could not have realized the awful tragedy about to be revealed to him.

"Yes, I did," Clark replied. "They're in there," and he pointed to the house.

Mr. and Mrs. Bailey soon discovered the awful truth, and then it was their turn to act quickly but safely. When the girls saw Mr. and Mrs. Bailey, they burst into tears and their cries for their mother and father were the most pitiful sound that ever fell on human ears.

Mr. Bailey turned his attention to the man with the gun. "Well, Roy," he said, "hadn't we better get somebody here?" He wanted to keep the demented man interested until he could get his gun.

"I reckon we had," Clark replied.

"Well, who do you think we had better get?" asked Mr. Bailey.

"Oh, some of the neighbors, I suppose," replied Clark.

Mrs. Bailey telephoned her sons to come over and other neighbors were notified. A short while later, Earl, the Baileys' eldest son, arrived. Earl and Roy, who had been associates and had frequently gone places together, looked into each other's eyes and exchanged a friendly greeting. Then Earl succeeded in doing the thing most all desired to be done.

"Say, Roy," Earl remarked, "there is going to be a lot of women along here in a few minutes and if they see you with a shotgun in your hands, they will be scared, and it won't look nice. Don't you think you had better throw the gun away, Roy?" he asked. Roy who seemed to be in a kind of daze, replied that he supposed he might as well, and with those words, he unloaded the magazine and tossed the gun on the grass. Still with rare presence of mind, no one tried to pick up the gun--not right then, at least. Then Roy tossed the loaded cartridges out on the grass and sat down to await the coming of the sheriff and other officials from Red Oak. While Roy's attention was diverted, one of the boys slipped around and picked up the gun, and they had the murderer in their power.

When Sheriff O.E. Jackson, accompanied by County Attorney W.C. Ratcliff and City Marshal Sam Davis of Red Oak arrived, the prisoner offered no resistance and told them it was not necessary to put handcuffs on him. He reiterated his repeated statement that he was perfectly sane, knew what he had done and regretted it. "I would give anything if I could bring back these girls' parents," he said. "I thought they had it in for me, but I was mistaken, I guess, and I am sorry."

And then occurred another little incident which threw more light on the man's disposition. For the first time since the tragedy, he showed fight when he beheld City Marshal Davis. It seemed that early the previous spring, Clark, who occasionally got drunk, had gone to Red Oak from Omaha and had been drinking freely. He called at the Griffith Inn and demanded the privilege of using the phone. Mr. Davis informed him that a party was using the phone at that time but said he could use it just as soon as the other man had finished. At this, it was said, Clark flew into a rage and became violently abusive, and the result was that Marshal Davis arrested him, put him in jail, and had him fined for disturbing the peace. Clark never got over what he called being needlessly imprisoned and when he saw the Red Oak marshal on the night of the brutal murders, he cried out, "And there's another man I want to get before I get through!" So violent for the moment did he become that Marshal Davis was asked to retire from his sight, which he did.

County Coroner A.L. Linquist from Stanton had been notified and arrived on the scene shortly after the call had gone out. When the excitement had subsided a little, it was deemed advisable to hold an inquest right away, and a jury composed of J.E. Bergstrom, Edward Bailey, and S.W. Altaffer was empaneled. The prisoner confessed his guilt, and the verdict of the jury was that Mr. and Mrs. John T. Bell came to their death by means of wounds inflicted by a shotgun in the hands of Roy Clark.

Clark was twenty-six years of age and not a bad-looking fellow. He was about five feet seven inches in height, weighed about 150 pounds. He had brown eyes, brown hair, and heavy eyebrows. He liked to have his booze occasionally, but he never let it get the better of him, and at the time of the tragedy, was perfectly sober. There was not the slightest odor of alcohol on his breath, and he said he had not been drinking. The incident at Red Oak involving Clark and the marshal simply showed how he could carry a grudge and nurse it until he really began to think he had been abused. His parents were well respected people living south of Creston, but Clark himself was not well known there, and not much of his real character was known until he committed the heinous deed that night. He had never committed any other crime.

After Clark's arrest, he was rushed to the Red Oak jail and placed in a cell. There was some talk of lynching, and no chances were taken on permitting the crowd to lay hands on the man, for the feeling of hatred was at a high pitch.

While in jail, Clark befriended a man by the name of George Baker, who had served seven years in Anamosa State Penitentiary for the killing of Claude Grice back in 1907 by hitting him on the head. Baker was paroled and recently pardoned. On November 26, 1914 he was said to have forged several checks on the name of Tom Kirby of Grant Township, Montgomery County, Iowa. He was caught before he had time to leave town and was in jail on $1,000 bail. By this time, Clark had been in prison three months awaiting his trial on December 15, 1914 when Baker suggested to Clark that he had a plan to escape and filled him in on all the details.

Roy Clark and George Baker made their escape from the Montgomery County Jail on Saturday night, December 5, 1914, by sawing two bars from the south window of the southeast cell room. Although a bloodhound traced the convicts' course to three miles northwest of Red Oak and descriptions of the men were sent to all the authorities within a radius of between fifty and a hundred miles, nothing was heard of the fugitives. That the men were aided by outside parties in their escape was entertained, without a doubt, by the county authorities and all others who were acquainted with the circumstances of the affair.

CRIME and CALAMITY

Clark and Baker made their escape almost under Sheriff Jackson's nose, and their timing of the affair was conclusive proof that the escape had been planned for some time and that they were assisted by others. Sheriff Jackson had taken their supper to them about 6 p.m., and everything appeared alright at that time. He did not see the prisoners as he shoved their food to them through the chuckhole that was used for this purpose. The sheriff stated that it was his custom to let the prisoners intermingle in the main room during the daytime but at night he locked Clark and Baker in the individual "St. Louis cakes" in different rooms. At 8 p.m. he had gone to the jail room from his home, which was built at the front of the jail, and was attached to it by a corridor, with the intention of locking them up for the night, when he made the discovery that they were gone. He had been at home the whole time after he had taken them their supper, until he went to lock them up.

The bars were sawed at the bottom and bent upwards, making a hole about twelve by sixteen inches, through which they crawled, reaching the window by standing on the radiator. They also sawed the upper clips of the heavy wire screen that was over the window on the outside, bending it down to the top of the high fence surrounding the jail building. This fence was between eight and ten feet high and was built four or five feet from the building. The screen was a net of one-half inch, made of heavy wire, and it afforded a strong platform for the men when they crawled from the window to the fence. An old snowplow that had been left in the alley behind the jail was moved up to the spot where the men jumped from the fence. A peculiar circumstance of the affair was that the streetlights in the west end of Red Oak were turned off at the time of their escape. The men were required to pass from the alley through several of the principal streets in Red Oak in making their getaway, and if it had not been for the absence of the streetlights, they might have been seen. Clark had made a complete change of his clothing before he made his escape, putting on a clean pair of underwear and T-shirt and clean socks, and changing his overalls to a clean suit of clothes which he had in jail with him. The dog took the scent from his discarded clothing. There were seven other prisoners in the jail at the time Clark and Baker made their escape, but all claimed they knew nothing of the affair when questioned by Sheriff O.E. Jackson.

A newspaper report in the *Adams County Free Press*, Corning, Iowa, dated December 26, 1914 stated that the two desperate criminals who escaped from the county jail at Red Oak were still at liberty. Countless rumors had been circulated as to their whereabouts, but most of them amounted to nothing. The B & Q freight crew claimed that they saw Clark jump off their train at Denver the day after their escape, and the authorities in that city claimed to have seen a man of Clark's description that day. Since that time, nothing more had been heard of the fugitives. Then there was a rumor in March 1915 that Clark had been taken from a train at Crawfordsville, Indiana but this seemed to have been without merit. Sheriff Jackson had received no word from there, regarding the man taken, nor had he received any information which would indicate that Clark had been apprehended.

The following is the statement which Clark made to Sheriff R.A. Dunn, Montgomery County Iowa in February 1918, telling of his escape from jail and life on the run as a fugitive:

> *Baker suggested to me that we would get out. Said he would have tools in a few days. A boy about 12-years-old handed them into us, wrapped and hidden in a magazine or newspaper. There were several saws of varied sizes, and I believe I could find one of them in the jail now, where I hid it. I hid one saw in the flush of the stool so that I could saw out again if they ever caught me and carried a piece of saw in my belt until I moved to Hanley Falls.*
>
> *Before Baker got in and before I got in, one of the bars had been sawed nearly in two, and I had taken my measurement so then I figured I could get out in short order if the trial did not go to suit me. That is, I was willing to take 10 or 20 years, but I didn't deserve a life sentence. I felt that 'life' was too much. Both of*

us used the hacksaws and nearly all the other boys in jail knew we were going. We put oil of mustard on our shoes before we went out so that the bloodhounds couldn't track us. Some knew Baker was going, some didn't. On the Saturday we left, we sawed all day on the U-bolts that secured the heavy screen to the outside of the bars. It was a dark and foggy evening and after supper Baker put on his overcoat and heavy trousers, and then I rode the screen from the window to the wall that is back of the jail, and I walked across the screen and dropped down on the outside. Now I remember, I didn't have time to put on my overalls, as I was afraid the jailer would smell the mustard, which was very strong. Baker said he would go east and I would go south. Baker ran across the schoolyard and I walked slowly toward the south. I met many people and spoke to some of them. I didn't go straight to the railroad track but would walk slowly a block and then zigzag. Now I remember, I didn't have time to put the mustard on my shoes while in the jail, but I put it on down in the railroad yard and threw the bottle into the weeds. I walked on the track part of the time and wagon road part of the time. Then I walked backwards so that my tracks would fool anyone who might be looking for me. Walked nearly all night and then crawled into a straw stack and stayed all the next day. Walked that night and crawled into a straw stack but came out for some-thing to eat. I had a lunch with me, but this was all gone, and I was hungry, so I went into the first house I came to and they gave me my breakfast. Then I started to walk but caught a ride with a man in a buggy who hauled me into, I think, Tabor. He gave me a pair of canvas gloves. Then I walked from Tabor to Hamburg, Iowa. There was no train at Hamburg, so I started on down the track on foot. I wanted to keep moving. Walked a station or two and then bought a ticket to St. Joseph, Missouri. Got a ticket and a train right away for Kansas City. Looked around in Kansas City one night and left there on the M.K.&T. buying a ticket with what money I had left. This took me to Oklahoma, I think. I was out of *money and tried to pawn my watch but couldn't get over a $3.00 loan on it, so I sold it to a one-armed man who runs a second-hand store for $4.00. Then I got something to eat and bummed out of town and landed in Muscovite, Oklahoma. My first stop to work was at Sherman, Texas where I went to work for Archer Bros. and I worked there until October of the next year. While I was there, I went to Sunday school every Sunday and Mr. Abbott was my Sunday school teacher. He was also superintendent of the Sunday school.*

I blew what money I had saved except $10 or $12 and went to Paris, Texas and worked my way from there to Waggoner, Illinois where I shucked corn for Joe Clark and Harry Lee. After corn shucking, I went to St. Louis had a good time and bought two guns as I was going to Minnesota to hunt and trap. Paid my way to Minneapolis and bought some traps there and went from there to International Falls, Minnesota where I trapped until July of the next year. I married Mildred Kjostrom (or Hillstrom) there on February 24, 1916. I couldn't make the trapping go, so I went to town and sold the guns. In July I left International Falls and went to Grand Forks, North Dakota worked through harvest and threshing. Then I went to Thompson, North Dakota and worked in a potato house. Went to Hanley Falls the 20th or 22nd of October 1916 and have been there ever since. I worked for E.P. Squire 8 or 9 months until stacking time. My wife went to Grand Forks to visit her sister, but she came back when I began shucking corn. I had rented a farm of 160 acres from Mr. Veldy for the next year.

For over three years, Clark had been successful in avoiding detection, but the worry brought on by his crime, and the constant fear that he would be picked up by the authorities, induced him to confide in his wife and a friend. Clark was glad to be back, and it was apparent to anyone who talked with him that he was relieved by his confession. Clark was in constant fear of arrest, and while at times he was cheerful and could get out and have a good time dancing and the like, the fact that he was a fugitive from justice was on his mind most of the time, and he often thought he was about to be taken. When he went hunting with friends in Minnesota, he fancied that some of them were detectives and expected to be shot in his tracks. Several times he was ready to give himself up to the authorities, but each time until the last, he had been prevented from doing so by the belief that officers were about to arrest him, before he could make a confession. This irritated him as he wanted to tell his story voluntarily, and he dreaded being taken by force. During his three years at large, he said he felt no bodily fear, but the danger of detection worried him. On the other hand, he said he had a constant feeling that those who were pursuing him were in fear of him. Only once while he was a fugitive, had he seen anyone he knew, until he was brought back here. That time was at Verdun, Illinois while he was hired out to a farmer as a corn picker. While they were talking, a man who Clark had known in Missouri came up to them, but Clark turned away to avoid recognition. Clark said nobody would ever know how badly he wanted to shake hands with that friend, but he dared not.

Roy Clark went to trial in Montgomery County in February 1918. The jury brought in a verdict declaring Clark insane. Judge Thomas Arthur at once sentenced the prisoner to be committed to the ward for the criminally insane in the Anamosa State Penitentiary on March 1, 1918 and there confined until his reason was restored, at which time he was to be returned to Montgomery County and tried on a charge of murder. Six ballots were required before the jury arrived at a verdict. The difficulty arose over the question as to whether the verdict should be based upon the testimony of the physicians or whether the jurors should make their decision on their own observation of the prisoner. Dr. Max E. White, superintendent of the state hospital for the insane at Clarinda, and four Red Oak physicians testified and gave as their opinions that Clark was insane. Clark sat with his eyes glued to the floor as the verdict was read and was not visibly affected when sentence was pronounced. His father, mother, and wife sat as spectators of the proceedings in a courtroom filled with an audience but showed no signs of emotion at the reading of the verdict or the sentence imposed. His wife took him by the arm as he passed from the courtroom and walked back to the jail with him.

On December 29, 1922, the insanity board reviewed Clark's case and it was their decision that Roy Clark would remain a prisoner in the insane ward of the state reformatory at Anamosa. Clark, now thirty-three years old, had recently asked for a trial to test his sanity. If proven sane, he would have been arrested on a charge of murder in the first degree. He never faced trial for the murder of John and Carrie Bell.

Roy Clark died in the insane asylum at the Anamosa State Penitentiary on September 8, 1925, from a skull fracture, having been hit in the head with a piece of pipe by another insane inmate. He was thirty-six years old and was buried in Riverside Cemetery in Anamosa. He was survived by his wife, Mildred, and parents, Leonard and Clara Clark.

Anamosa State Penitentiary at Anamosa Iowa
Present day aerial view of prison complex

(photo from asphistory.com)

CRIME and CALAMITY

Construction of the Anamosa State Penitentiary started in 1872 and continued until 1943 by inmates, using limestone from quarries in Stone City a few miles away. It was constructed from "Anamosa Limestone" in the style of a castle inspiring the nickname, "The White Palace of the West." The walls stretched 900 feet across the front and 800 feet along the sides. Some walls were 24 feet tall and nearly 8 feet thick at the base. The walls go 17 or 18 feet into the ground to prevent prisoners from digging their way out. It is a maximum-security prison that housed some of the most hardened criminals in the state. It was once home to John Wayne Gacy and Robert Hansen, both serial killers. The enormous structure sits on 15 acres of beautifully manicured lawns and gardens and houses as many as 1,200 male inmates. The prison is still in use today and is listed on the National Historic Register.

Insane Ward at Anamosa
where Clark was incarcerated
This building was torn down in 1930s
to make room for new living units
(Photo History Archive, Anamosa State Penitentiary)

Roy L. Clark's Marker
Riverside Cemetery, Anamosa, IA
(photo from "Billion Grave")

John & Carrie Bell's Monument
Macedonia Cemetery, Ft. Leonard Wood, MO
(photo from "Find a Grave")

CRIME and CALAMITY

BURGLARS BLOW SAFE
AT ST. LEO

ST. LEO WAS a little inland town situated on the line between Omro and Burton townships. It had a population of nearly 200 people at one time. The village was named in honor of Pope Leo. Homesteaders settled in the area as early as 1878, and in January 1880 a country post office named St. Leo was established. Valentine Lenz was the postmaster and the office was at his farm house on section 32, Omro. In 1900 Jacob Geib platted the townsite on the southeast quarter of section 32. At one time, St. Leo had prospects of being a boom town.

At 3:30 a.m. on November 1, 1921, St. Leo residents heard a light explosion in the town proper. Many thought it was the leftover prank from a Halloween celebration and did not know that it had occurred at the bank in town. A brief time later, another explosion was heard. The whole door of a safe was blown off, and parts of it blew

through the front door of the bank building and landed in the street. The entire front of the building was wrecked and the interior damaged. Immediately after the second explosion, residents were in the street and saw men running toward an automobile parked two blocks from the bank. The men made good their escape. No one had time to secure the license number, describe the car, or learn how many men were involved in the robbery. The bandits' car headed east out of town at a high rate of speed. No one tailed them, but all the neighboring towns were notified. The bandits blew the safe of the First State Bank of St. Leo and escaped with several thousand dollars in securities and about $100 in cash. The securities were worthless, according to cashier, L.P. Funke, but there may have been a few liberty bonds in the safety deposit boxes. The bandits succeeded in blowing only the outer door of the safe. Most of the bank's cash was within the inner door and was untouched. Nothing more was reported in the newspapers about this crime, and no one was apprehended.

Early Wednesday morning, November 14, 1923, bank burglars made the second attempt in two years to loot the First State Bank of St. Leo, and like the first time in November 1921, they left the bank without obtaining any money for their labors. From all indications, it was a well-planned and coolly executed piece of work, despite the unsuccessful outcome of their efforts.

At 2 a.m., a loud detonation awakened some of the residents and was shortly followed by another blast. Father Kotouc, whose residence was directly across the road from the bank, was among the first to be aroused. Kotouc switched on the porch and upstairs lights, which shone like a spotlight on the front of the bank. The two lookouts were pacing back and forth at the front entrance. Kotouc also pounded on his window, but they paid no attention. An effort was made to use a telephone to call the authorities at Canby and Granite Falls, but it was

CRIME and CALAMITY

found that the telephone wires had been cut, completely isolating the town from outside communication. The burglars continued their work in a cool and unhurried manner, and after the first two heavy explosions, there were five more shots at regular intervals. The last one came at about 3:15 a.m., an hour and fifteen minutes after the first shot. Shortly after the last charge had exploded at the bank, some wide-eyed residents felt brave enough and quietly sneaked up in the shadow of the bank as close as they dared. They were just in time to overhear the burglars discussing the possibility of making a similar attempt on the Farmers State Bank of St. Leo, which was just a half a block east of the First State Bank, but after a few moments' consultation, they decided to abandon that project for another time. Then a car drove up to the bank, and four men exited the building and entered the vehicle. The car headed east toward Clarkfield and rapidly disappeared.

Inspection of the bank the following morning revealed the fact that the burglars gained entrance to the building by smashing one of the two front windows. The other one was broken out, evidently by the force of the concussion from the blast or fragments of flying metal. The heavy safe doors had been blown from their hinges, and particles of broken steel from the safe were found embedded in the wall of the bank room, and other fragments of steel were blown clear through the ceiling and through the roof of the building. A steel chisel was found still tightly wedged between the two inner doors of the safe where it had been left by the burglars after their vain attempt to force open the inner door. The inner compartment of the safe contained $300 in currency.

Shortly before dawn, Vincent Jelen of St. Leo reported seeing a touring car containing five men who answered to the description of the burglars. The men slowed up as he approached them and looked sharply at him as his car passed theirs but did not stop.

The safe, which was badly damaged, was a new one installed less than two years ago to replace the one wrecked by burglars in 1921. Nitroglycerine was used to blow the safe, and pieces of soap used in the process were found on the floor.

Manager Harrington of the telephone company, along with a crew of linemen, were busy the next day making repairs to the telephone wires into St. Leo. The wires had been cut by the burglars in three directions -- east, west and south -- before attempting their bank job.

The St. Leo blacksmith shop had been broken into probably just before the attempt on the bank. It appeared the burglars might have searched for an acetylene torch to be used to cut into the safe, but none was found. Other tools were scattered about. Many people believed that the nitroglycerine was in the hands of well-experienced safecrackers and this was not done by amateurs.

Officials of the bank were advised not to attempt to open the safe because of the possibility that some undischarged nitroglycerine left in the safe might be accidentally detonated and cause injury to someone. Cashier L.P. Funke was again witness to another attempted bank robbery in St. Leo just two years after the first attempt. An insurance company representative arrived at the bank later that week, inspected the premises, and filed the report. Repairs were made to the building, and another safe door was installed. Again, no one was arrested for the crime.

Bank robberies were everyday occurrences in the 1920s, and no one seemed to ever get caught for the crime. There were "gangs" of safecrackers and bank robbers. These men were called "yeggs" or "yeggmen." In September 1924, Charles Brown, head of the protective department of the Minnesota Bankers Association, ascribed to I.W.W. sabotage the series of bank robberies which averaged "a bank a day" in Minnesota, Wisconsin, Iowa, and the Dakotas. Mobs, unequalled in size and daring in the history of the northwest, were described in a warning issued by Brown to bankers of the five states. Investigation by the Minnesota Bankers Association had revealed that there were several subordinate mobs of from four to six members, each working under the direction of a central clearing house and staged with the finest precision. First, the chief located the banks and the towns and instructed one of the mobs to pull the job at a certain hour, on a certain day, usually late at night. Then, armed with automatic pistols, shotguns, and rifles, they proceeded to terrorize the inhabitants of the town after first cutting all telegraph, telephone, and power line communications, isolating the town. The bank was then taken by force, the safe blown open with nitroglycerine, money and valuables taken, and then the bank interior was wrecked. To further intimidate the residents, "yeggs" used revolvers and pistols, and fired at buildings recklessly.

Reports from the association had it that two mobs were under surveillance in the Twin Cities area and one of them was surrounded in a house in St. Paul. Police were called in to assist with the arrest, but the "yeggs" made good their escape. One of the mobs was said to be from Chicago and one from Iowa, using the same methods, operating simultaneously, and each knowing the other one's plans. During this time, many "yeggs" remained in the bank-robbing business their entire lives. It was a profitable endeavor, and the chances of getting caught were quite slim.

ACKNOWLEDGMENTS

For me, writing a book is a long, arduous journey leading to many twists and turns along the way. It is a very exciting experience for all the history discovered and the many amazing people you meet. The writer of any book is just one small part of this major undertaking, and it can never be accomplished without the assistance of many dedicated people volunteering their time and talent in helping uncover forgotten stories from the past. Every piece of information discovered is a real treasure that is truly cherished and helps bring the story to life. I am never on this journey alone and have so many amazing people to thank for their commitment in documenting forgotten history. So much appreciation and gratitude must be extended to Debra Gangelhoff, an amazing research specialist, who dedicated so much of her time searching for stories in old newspapers and court documents at the MN History Center. This was such a great help to me, and I couldn't have done it without her. To my dear friend, Michelle Gatz, who encourages me to keep writing great stories from the past. Thank you, Michelle, for sharing files with me so I could write these wonderful stories. Thank you, Ashley Finnes, for copying many articles from the

Granite Falls Tribune newspaper. A big thank you to all those great people who helped provide information and assistance in some way, your dedication is appreciated – Debbie Joramo, Darla Gebhard, Jan Louwagie, Laurie Johnson and Amy Christianson. To my copy editor, Joan Rogers, thank you for another great job of editing the manuscript, and thanks to all the staff at Outskirts Press who helped in the publishing process. And to all my readers, thank you for your support and passion for history. I hope you enjoy the book.

ABOUT THE AUTHOR

I was born and raised in Echo, Yellow Medicine County. My parents were John and Lorraine Larsen, who settled in the tiny village in 1950 after they were married. I am the oldest of eight children. Echo was a prosperous town when I grew up, however, many of the buildings have since been demolished. The tiny village still maintains its special history and unique charm. Echo Granite Works is one of the main businesses still operating. The monument business was started by my grandfather, Thor, and father, John, in 1950. It is now owned by my brothers, Daniel and David Larsen. All the gravestones are beautifully hand-crafted and one-of-a-kind masterpieces.

After I graduated, I spent several years in Minneapolis before moving to California. I received a Bachelor of Arts degree with a major in Interdisciplinary Studies from the University of California. In 2005, I returned to Minnesota and live in the small town of Belview, four miles from my childhood home.

My career brought me into the fascinating world of long-lost history. I have been the Director of the Yellow Medicine County and Redwood County museums. I have since retired and enjoy researching and writing books that document Minnesota history. This is my third book. My other books are titled "Murder in Gales, A Rose Hanged Twice" and "Murder, Mystery, and Mayhem in Minnesota."

Thanks to all those people out there who enjoy reading my books and are passionate about history. The books are available at Outskirts Press, Amazon, Barnes & Noble, and other book distributors.

Visit my website at www.outskirtspress.com/CrimeandCalamity

Patricia Lubeck

REFERENCES

INTRODUCTION

1. History of Yellow Medicine County, Arthur P. Rose, pub. 1914, pgs. 88, 139, 161
2. Granite Falls 1879-1979, Carl & Amy Narvestad, pub. 1979, pgs. 90-93

BATTLE OF WOOD LAKE

1. History of Yellow Medicine County, Arthur P. Rose, pub. 1914, pgs. 64-70

SHOT BY ACCIDENT

1. "The Willmar Homicide," Star Tribune, Mpls., MN, May 19, 1871, pg. 4
2. "Trial of Coney," Star Tribune, Mpls., MN, December 14, 1871, pg. 4
3. "The Oldest Man in Prison," Star Tribune, Mpls., MN,

February 2, 1885, pg. 3

4. "A Bill for a Pardon," Star Tribune, Mpls., MN, February 22, 1885, pg. 3

5. "Out at Last," St. Paul Globe, St. Paul, MN, January 25, 1887, pg. 3

6. State of MN vs. Richard B. Coney, grand jury indictment, September 20, 1871

BLIZZARDS, GRASSHOPPERS AND PRAIRIE FIRES

1. History of Yellow Medicine County, Arthur P. Rose, pub. 1914, pgs. 106-118, 270-272

GOLD IN GRANITE FALLS

1. "Gold Mining in Granite," Granite Falls 1879-1979, Carl & Amy Narvestad, pub. 1979, pgs. 30-31

2. "Our Mines and Mineral Wealth," Granite Falls Tribune, December 11, 1888, pg. 1

3. "Thompson in the Mines," Granite Falls Tribune, May 14, 1889, pg. 1

4. "Gold is King!" Granite Falls Tribune, June 11, 1889, pg. 1

5. "The Last Assay," Granite Falls Tribune, June 25, 1889, pg. 1

6. "The Ben Harrison a Bird," Granite Falls Tribune, July 2, 1889, pg. 1

7. "Ben is Rich," Granite Falls Tribune, July 9, 1889, pg. 1

8. "A Human Fiend," Granite Falls Tribune, June 30, 1896, pg. 4 & 5

9. "The Jensvold Boy," Granite Falls Tribune, July 7, 1896, pg. 4

10. "The Boy Beater," Granite Falls Tribune, July 14, 1896, pg. 5

11. "Court Notes," Granite Falls Tribune, January 19, 1897, pg. 4

12. "Court is Over," Granite Falls Journal, March 25, 1897, pg. 5

TEXAS JACK

1. "That Jail Delivery," Daily Globe, St. Paul, MN, May 11, 1881, pg. 2
2. "Texas Jack," New Ulm Review, New Ulm, MN, May 25, 1881, pg. 2
3. "A Reward," Daily Globe, St. Paul, MN, May 11, 1881, pg. 2

MYSTERIOUS DEATH

1. "Death of Clarence P. Cook," Granite Falls Tribune, June 16, 1885, pg. 1
2. "Fatal Accident," The Rochester Post, Rochester, MN, June 19, 1885, pg. 2
3. "C.P. Cook," Granite Falls Tribune, June 30, 1885, pg. 4

HALF AN OUNCE OF ARSENIC

1. "Death by Violence," Granite Falls Tribune, July 28, 1885, pg. 1
2. "Poisoning at Granite Falls," News Messenger, Marshall, MN, July 31, 1885, pg. 3
3. "Preliminary Examination of Mrs. Purvis," Granite Falls Tribune, August 18, 1885, pg. 1
4. "Sentence Pronounced," Granite Falls Tribune, December 8, 1885, pg. 1
5. State of MN vs. Sarah Purvis, grand jury indictment, October 1885
6. "Board of Pardons, State of MN," January 3, 1898
7. "Clerk Dies of Injuries in Robbery," Kalamazoo Gazette, Kalamazoo, MI, January 13, 1972, pg. 1

A Crime of Incest

1. State of MN vs. Ole Narkin, grand jury indictment, May 1885
2. "Sentence Pronounced," Granite Falls Tribune, December 8, 1885, pg. 1
3. "A Wife's Missive," Granite Falls Tribune, December 8, 1885, pg. 4
4. Ole O. Narkin vs. Martha Narkin, divorce transcript, April 20, 1891

Firecracker Starts an Inferno

1. "Fearful Fireworks," Granite Falls Tribune, July 9, 1889

Father Shoots his Son

1. "Killed his Son," Reform Advocate, Granite Falls, MN, November 1, 1893, pg. 1
2. "Murder," Granite Falls Journal, November 2, 1893, pg. 1
3. "An Awful Deed!" Granite Falls Tribune, November 7, 1893, pg. 1
4. "Held for Murder," Granite Falls Tribune, November 14, 1893, pg. 1
5. "Held for Murder!" The Canby News, Canby, MN, November 17, 1893, pg. 1
6. "Attempted Suicide," Granite Falls Tribune, January 4, 1894
7. "The Murder Case," Granite Falls Tribune, January 16, 1894, pg. 5
8. "He Got Six," Granite Falls Tribune, March 6, 1894, pg. 1
9. "The Baierl Case," Granite Falls Journal, March 8, 1894, pg. 1
10. "Anton Baierl Called to Heavenly Slumber," The Canby Press, Canby, MN, May 19, 1927, pg. 1

11. State of MN vs. Anton Baierl, trial transcript, December 21, 1893
12. Parole of Anton Baierl on June 23, 1898

A STABBING AFFAIR

1. "Intended to Kill Him," Canby News, Canby, MN, September 18, 1896, pg. 1
2. "Guilty of Murder," Canby News, Canby, MN, September 25, 1896, pg. 1
3. "Harry DeVere," Granite Falls Tribune, January 26, 1897
4. State of MN vs. Harry DeVere, trial transcript, October 3, 1896

A DRUNKEN BRAWL

1. "Cold in Death," Granite Falls Tribune, January 12, 1897, pg. 4
2. "Court is Over, Olson gets Eight Years," Granite Falls Journal, March 25, 1897, pg. 5
3. State of MN vs. Austin Olson, trial transcript, January 9, 1897
4. "Board of Pardons, State of MN," January 8, 1900

DEATH IN A BURNING BARN

1. "Cremated!" Reform Advocate, Clarkfield, MN, October 21, 1897, pg. 1
2. "Burning of Sivert Berg's Barn," Granite Falls Tribune, October 26, 1897, pg. 4
3. "Four Men Burned," The Princeton Union, Princeton, MN, October 28, 1897, pg. 3

BEATEN WITH A BILLY

1. "The Echo Murder," Minneapolis Journal, Mpls., MN, May 20, 1898
2. "Murder!" Granite Falls Tribune, May 24, 1898, pg. 2
3. "Killed by her Husband," New Ulm Review, New Ulm, MN, May 25, 1898, pg. 1
4. "Foully Murdered," Reform Advocate, Clarkfield, MN, May 26, 1898, pg. 1
5. "Murder near Echo," The Redwood Gazette, Redwood Falls, MN, May 26, 1898, pg. 1
6. "Murder!" The Canby News, Canby, MN, May 27, 1898
7. "To be Hanged," The Canby News, Canby, MN, July 7, 1898
8. "October 20th," Granite Falls Tribune, October 4, 1898
9. "The Gallows Ready," Granite Falls Tribune, October 18, 1898, pg. 1
10. "Ott is Hanged," Star Tribune, Mpls., MN, October 20, 1898, pg. 1
11. "Ott Hung," Granite Falls Tribune, October 25, 1898, pg. 1
12. "The Execution," The Canby News, Canby, MN, October 28, 1898
13. "Dropped to Death," Sleepy Eye newspaper, October, 1898
14. "Not Proud of his Title," Star Tribune, Mpls., MN, January 26, 1903, pg. 7
15. "Makes him Pay Board Bill," Little Falls Herald, Little Falls, MN, June 25, 1909, pg. 1
16. "American House," Little Falls Herald, Little Falls, MN, November 5, 1909, pg. 12
17. State of MN vs. Joseph Ott, trial transcript, June 21, 1898

POISON AND A PAIR OF SCISSORS

1. "Suicide," Reform Advocate, Clarkfield, MN, June 16, 1898, pg. 1

2. "County Coroner J.W. Donnell Commits Suicide," Granite Falls Tribune, June 1898, pg. 1

POKER GAME GONE BAD

1. "Rough Usage, This," The Saint Paul Globe, St. Paul, MN, December 4, 1896, pg. 4
2. "Poker Ends in Shooting," The Saint Paul Globe, St. Paul, MN, April 16, 1901, pg. 3
3. "Shot him Twice," Renville Record, Renville, MN, April 17, 1901, pg. 1
4. "Wages of Sin is Death," The Saint Paul Globe, St. Paul, MN, April 17, 1901, pg. 3
5. "A Surprise and a Tragedy," Renville Star Farmer, Renville, MN, April 19, 1901, pg. 1
6. "Fatally Shot," Denison Review, Denison, IA, April 22, 1901, pg. 1
7. "Buried by the Eagles," Denison Bulletin, Denison, IA, April 22, 1901
8. "A Jury Denounced," Minneapolis Journal, Mpls., MN, July 1, 1901, pg. 5
9. "Wintner Free," Renville Record, Renville, MN, July 3, 1901
10. "Verdict of Acquittal," Renville Star Farmer, Renville, MN, July 5, 1901, pg. 1
11. "Volstead Vindicated," Minneapolis Journal, Mpls., MN, July 5, 1901, pg. 8
12. "Arrested in Brooklyn," The Saint Paul Globe, St. Paul, MN, August 26, 1901, pg. 2
13. "Attempted Suicide," Detroit Free Press, Detroit, MI, August 13, 1874, pg. 1
14. "The Park Suicide," Detroit Free Press, Detroit, MI, August 14, 1874, pg. 1
15. "Poker History," www.twincitiespoker.com and www.

pokerplayernewspaper.com

16. State of MN vs. Sigmund Wintner, trial transcript, April 29, 1901

Raided the "Blind Pig"

1. "Raided the Blind Pig," Reform Advocate, Clarkfield, MN, September 26, 1901, pg. 1

Strange Disappearance

1. "What's Become of City Engineer Gehbauer," Canby Advocate, Canby, MN, January 12, 1917, pg. 1
2. "Engineer Gehbauer Lost, Strayed or Stolen," Granite Falls Tribune, January 16, 1917, pg. 1
3. "Engineer Gehbauer Gone," Granite Falls Journal, January 18, 1917, pg. 1

Gambling in a Box Car

1. "Hanley Falls Has Shooting Affray," Granite Falls Tribune, December 26, 1916, pg. 1
2. "Johnson Not Guilty in Shooting Affray," Granite Falls Tribune, January 23, 1917, pg. 1

Froze to Death

1. "Hanley Doctor Loses Life in Blizzard," Granite Falls Tribune, February 6, 1917, pg. 1

Train Wreck near Echo

1. "Wreck on the St. Louis near Echo," Echo Enterprise, date unknown

2. "Railroad," Echo, 1892 to 2017, pgs. 40-41

JUSTIFIABLE HOMICIDE

1. "Former Graniteite Shot by Montana Sheriff," Granite Falls Tribune, February 6, 1917, pg. 1

COMMITTED AS INSANE

1. "Red Oak Farmhand Killed Parents of Girl," The Courier, Waterloo, IA, August 25, 1914, pg. 9
2. "Two Persons Killed by Crazed Farmhand," The Sioux County Index, Hull, IA, August 28, 1914, pg. 6
3. "Slayer of Two Breaks Jail at Red Oak, IA," The Courier, Waterloo, IA, December 9, 1914, pg. 7
4. "Confesses Double Murder at Red Oak," Evening Times-Republican, Marshalltown, IA, February 2, 1918, pg. 1
5. "Man Committed as Insane, Proves Murderer," Granite Falls Tribune, February 5, 1918, pg. 1
6. "Murderer is Located," Adams County Free Press, Corning, IA, February 9, 1918, pg. 3
7. "Murderer is Back," Adams County Free Press, Corning, IA, February 16, 1918, pg. 5
8. "Roy Clark Murder Trial," Adams County Free Press, Corning, IA, February 27, 1918, pg. 1
9. "Double Murderer Declared Insane," Evening Times-Republican, Marshalltown, IA, March 4, 1918, pg. 2
10. "Clark Escapes Murder Trial," The Des Moines Register, Des Moines, IA, December 30, 1922, pg. 2

BURGLARS BLOW SAFE AT ST. LEO

1. "Auto Bandits Blow Bank Safe of St. Leo Bank," The Brainerd Daily Dispatch, Brainerd, MN, November 1, 1921, pg. 1

2. "Five Bandits Calmly Loot St. Leo Bank," The Minneapolis. Star, Mpls., MN, November 14, 1923, pg. 1
3. "Foiled Bank Bandits Make Good Escape," Star Tribune, Mpls., MN, November 15, 1923, pg. 1
4. "Bank Burglars Blow Safe at St. Leo," Granite Falls Tribune, November 16, 1923, pg. 1

CPSIA information can be obtained
at www.ICGtesting.com
Printed in the USA
FFHW022235271018
49015980-53294FF